Philomène Grandin is a Swedish actress, scriptwriter and television host who has starred in a variety of films, TV series and theatre productions at the Stockholm and Gothenburg City Theatres. *Don't Forget Me* is her first book.

DON'T FORGET ME

A GRIPPING FAREWELL TO A REMARKABLE FATHER

PHILOMÈNE GRANDIN

TRANSLATED BY EDWARD BROMBERG

SCRIBNER

LONDON NEW YORK SYDNEY TORONTO NEW DELHI

First published in Great Britain by Scribner,
an imprint of Simon & Schuster UK Ltd, 2022

This edition published in Great Britain by Scribner,
an imprint of Simon & Schuster UK Ltd, 2023

1 3 5 7 9 10 8 6 4 2

Simon & Schuster UK Ltd
1st Floor
222 Gray's Inn Road
London WC1X 8HB

www.simonandschuster.co.uk
www.simonandschuster.com.au
www.simonandschuster.co.in

Simon & Schuster Australia, Sydney
Simon & Schuster India, New Delhi

A CIP catalogue record for this book is available from the British Library

Paperback ISBN: 978-1-3985-1140-8
eBook ISBN: 978-1-3985-1139-2

Typeset in Bembo by M Rules
Printed and Bound in the UK using 100% Renewable
Electricity at CPI Group (UK) Ltd

MIX
Paper | Supporting
responsible forestry
FSC
www.fsc.org
FSC® C171272

2016

'Your dad asked me to call. It's full of journalists here. It might be a good idea if you come as fast as possible.'

'Why? What's wrong?'

'Bob Dylan got the Nobel Prize.'

I leave my lunch untouched on the kitchen table. A brush of mascara and then I cycle as fast as I can. Ten minutes later I'm pedalling up Wollmar Yxkullsgatan. From a distance I see a small queue forming outside the store. It's not a store really, more a space where Papa arranges concerts one or two times a week or sits drinking coffee with his friends. I rip off my helmet before I reach the crest of the hill. Park my bike outside the store: peering through the window I see Papa already flanked by two of his neighbours. Guardian angels. 'Here comes the daughter. Let her through.' I enter the store feeling embarrassed by the importance I'm given. They explain that they've drawn up a list of who goes first and that the journalists are waiting outside until it's their turn. Papa is sitting on his throne in front of the computer, a tall desk chair upholstered in black leather. It's actually not a desk chair; it's a barber's chair, one of those you can pump up and down with your foot, another present from his friends and acquaintances. On his head he sports a sun hat, even though it's mid-October. Oblivious to the flashing cameras and the glare of television lights, he has a friendly greeting for everyone who enters. Reporter after reporter is granted an audience. They plant snares, trying to make him say something nasty about Dylan. But he sidesteps all their traps, he jokes, compares their cameras, loudly shouting in American English:

'Which one of you has the biggest? Which one of you is smartest?'

His broad New York Jewish accent fills the room. I recognize his humour. I pass through to the small kitchenette at the back of the store, search for a glass among the litter of folk-music magazines, compact discs and papers cohabiting the shelf with kitchen utensils. Finally I find one that is not too dirty. I fill it with water from the basin in the toilet. Trying not to breathe through my nose. Like the rest of the store, the walls of this tiny WC are covered with paintings and posters. Above the toilet is a framed note I scrawled as a teenager: 'Gentlemen are requested to lift the toilet seat when peeing.' A vintage 1980s pink paper clip is fixed to one corner of the note. The soles of my shoes stick to the floor.

I re-enter the makeshift film studio, pass the overflowing bookshelves and hand Papa the glass. I'm rewarded with a smacking kiss on the cheek.

'This is my daughter. I'd never survive without her!'

In the middle of all this commotion the landline rings. The Swedish Academy wants Dylan's number. The woman calling, she might have said that her name was Sara, speaks in a dry, terse tone, like the worst sort of journalist. She wants the phone number and she wants it now. I ask her to call back in five minutes. She refuses to hang up. I throw the receiver down, start riffling through ancient address books and email messages. I scan all the phone numbers Papa has scrawled in thick black felt-tip pen on the wall. I open drawer after drawer in the counter built along one of the walls, the one piece of furniture left over from the days when milk and dairy products were sold here. I find some contact information but it's full of odd number sequences. Papa is busy with the journalists, angry now that they insist on asking their questions in English:

'Forty years I've been living here, I can speak Swedish!'

Though actually he's jumping between the two languages at random.

A couple of minutes later the woman from the academy is on the phone again and I still haven't found what she's looking for. Papa hears the call and gets irritated at the constant interruptions. He shouts:

'Tell them to fuck off!'

Once more I put down the phone as I hear him tell his story for the hundredth time:

'Dylan walked into the store, same as everyone else. He picked up a guitar, started playing and then we became friends. I think it took about thirteen minutes. He wrote two songs for me!'

Papa takes a gulp of water:

'I was the first one to let him play a big hall. That's why he trusted me. When I rented Carnegie Hall people said to me: "Izzy! Are you crazy?"'

He mimics their wide eyes and gaping mouths:

'But I just said, "This kid is the best I've ever heard." And I don't joke about those things.'

Finally, all the journalists' questions have been answered. Also, I've located the right contact information for Dylan's manager. I send it in a text message to the woman from the academy. Twenty-four hours later Dylan still hasn't responded. No one knows if he intends to accept the prize or not. The man is silent. The Swedish Academy tells *Dagens Nyheter*, Sweden's major daily, that they were finally able to reach Dylan's manager. Supposedly he told them that 'he had no idea if, or when, the artist would acknowledge the prize'. Apparently, Dylan was napping before a concert when the prize was announced and was not to be woken.

Papa, on the other hand, was up at six in the morning for a live interview on Swedish national radio. He managed to set his alarm, dress himself and go downstairs to the street in time to catch the taxi. He can do it, when he needs to.

I'm eating breakfast with the children and turn the radio on. One of the old kind, a box with dials and an antenna. It lives on the windowsill sharing space with kids' drawings, old newspapers and ripening fruit. Natasha, my daughter, crunches cornflakes and feeds her teddy. I run a hand over her cheek. So soft and round. She's named after a character I played in a production of *War and Peace* many years ago. My golden-curled son, Nikolai, taps his phone. Soon he'll rush out the door on his way to school. He's grown too big for cuddling. Lasse is grinding coffee beans. When they whirl through the blades it sounds like the kitchen is about to explode. I lean in to the radio to hear Papa's gravelly voice, just in time to catch the radio host asking:

'So, Izzy, what do you think about Dylan getting the Nobel Prize?' He answers without hesitation:

'He should have got it thirty years ago!'

I sigh with relief. The whole interview could have been a disaster.

An hour later I meet Papa at the store. He stands leaning against the doorpost, waiting for me. He's calm but eager for a coffee. Arm in arm we walk to our favourite coffee shop on St Paulsgatan. On high bar stools we sit side by side next to the window. Looking out. Watching people passing by. I rub his back and feel the warmth. He's smaller now. He who used to be the biggest.

1980

I'm six years old and we're lying in the grass in a nearby park, Mariatorget. As we often do. Papa's dark-blue suit jacket is spread out under us. He lies on his stomach, writing with tiny letters in his journal. I lean my head on his back and look in my comic book. You can buy them for two kronor each at the store around the corner. They look almost as good as new. The grass tickles my arms and legs.

We lie there like that for an hour, maybe two. Sometimes I run across to the swings or dip my feet in the fountain. Other times I nod off, or Papa does. Then he shakes out his jacket and we walk to the store.

The store. The centre. Papa's place. There's always been *the store* ever since I was a baby. Our second home, Papa's workspace. He taps on the typewriter, cuts and pastes text and photos into his folk-music newsletter. Page 1, 2, 3, 4. I draw. There are books about folk music. Everywhere. Papa's library. Ceiling-high bookshelves. The walls covered with photographs and concert posters. Scissors, tape and glue stick. He snips articles from all the Swedish newspapers, and foreign papers when he can get them. He glues them on to blank sheets of paper, scribbles the date and files them in loose-leaf binders. There are binders for folk music, for Dylan, for the war in Cambodia, for the conflict between Israel and Palestine. I make my own magazine, borrow Papa's pens, sticky with glue, his light box and his rulers.

Papa often props the door open with the Golden Boot he won, a prize awarded by *Dagens Nyheter*. I don't really know why he got it. Something to do with folk music probably, something about the store. It looks like a beat-up Charlie Chaplin boot, unglued at the sole with nails sticking up. It's made of gold; even the shoelaces are golden. I like to carry it around. It weighs several kilos.

People come in sometimes. Usually older men. They ask about some record or book, or they ask if it's true that Papa knows Bob Dylan. Papa sighs. He doesn't have much for sale, a few records, an odd instrument, but they should at least buy his newsletter. It only costs five kronor.

'You should be supporting me!'

If they don't buy anything, he throws them out and we watch as they scuttle down the street in shock.

Three huge storefront windows look out on to the pavement and the enormous tree on the corner that gives us shade in the summer.

2016

I'm sitting on a chair in a stranger's kitchen. I put my make-up on attempting to look natural, just a shade prettier than usual. The man making the documentary about Papa wants the apartment he's rented to seem as if it's mine. I try to look relaxed, sitting by the kitchen window with a cup of coffee. I pull my legs up under me, trying to look bohemian in my black dress.

The film-maker sits perched by the camera a couple of metres away. He talks unceasingly, wants to film me backlit. I ask if I won't just become a silhouette then. He answers in perfect British English that his super-expensive camera will fix it. Will fix everything. He presses the record button:

'So, tell me about your father's store in New York.'

I don't know all the names of everyone who played in Papa's store sixty years ago. Also, my English deteriorates when I get nervous. I'm tracing the rim of the coffee cup with my finger, the palms of my hands are all sweaty.

The film-maker isn't satisfied with my answers. He starts

dictating what I should say, spells things out and wants me to memorize lines. I sit straight up, trying to rattle off names as if it were common knowledge that they played there:

'Joan Baez, Joni Mitchell, Bob Dylan, Emmylou Harris, Pete Seeger, Mississippi John Hurt, Patti Smith and ... um ... loads of other musicians and poets. They all used to perform at the Folklore Center.'

I notice how the words come out garbled.

'It was like a ... mecca for folk music in Greenwich Village.'

Two hours later I've repeated a litany of facts on demand. I related how Papa was born in 1928 in the Bronx and how his parents emigrated to the USA from Poland. With feigned enthusiasm I told the story of how Papa opened his store in New York at the end of the fifties. I described Bob Dylan, sitting at Papa's old typewriter, tapping out lyrics to his songs.

I clear my throat:

'But one day Papa had a visit from some Swedish folk musicians, Björn Ståbi and Bror Hjorth. They became friends. He developed an infatuation for Swedish folk music. It was that love, along with his hatred of the war in Vietnam, that made my parents move to Sweden in 1973. I was born a year later.'

The film-maker shuffles his notes. I believe that my parents' break-up, shortly after my birth, is not something he would be interested in so I don't mention it. Neither do I describe the way I lived one life with my mother and an entirely different one with my father.

We're finally done. I'm released out on to Mariatorget. I wipe the palms of my hands on my dress, fill my lungs with fresh air and look up at an open blue sky.

1981

Stockholm is moving slower; the summer holidays are here. Papa and I are sitting on a bench in Björns Trädgård, a city park paved with warm, grey asphalt. We sit opposite one another, two benches with a table in between. Papa has bought a half-litre block of ice cream. Nougat and vanilla. It's cheaper and perhaps even tastier than ice creams on sticks. He's brought with him two teaspoons and a knife from the cutlery drawer at home. All badly cleaned. He takes them now from his jacket pocket. Measuring the block, he meticulously performs the holy tradition of dividing the ice cream equally.

Papa, in deep concentration, saws through the ice cream. The carton frays at the cut edges. Once divided, he sets the two pieces next to each other so that we can see if he's cut fairly. He's almost always proud of the result. He's the phenomenal son of a baker 'from the Bronx' who learned as a child how to cut loaves of bread in precise and equal slices. The baker's son who on early mornings, in a New York bakery misty with flour, tossed hot loaves, fresh from the oven, to his little brother.

The ice cream is soft. It took a few minutes to walk from the grocery store to the park. Only Papa and I are here, and a few stubborn pigeons. Stockholm's other residents have probably left town for summer cottages.

We eat in reverent silence. Scrape our silver spoons against the smooth interior of the carton. Nothing should be wasted. Ice cream oozes from the side of the carton. Sticky. Delicious. Always a drop on Papa's shirt or trousers.

This is our day's adventure, the high point, what the loose change in Papa's pockets allows. On a day that we can splurge we might buy a lottery ticket at the food store. The one with little flaps that you bend up to see if you have the right numbers. We don't win very often, but it's always exciting. If we do win, five kronor perhaps, the day will turn out completely differently. We can afford to buy something more, something different.

Even though we don't own a car we sometimes buy a parking ticket. You buy them from a machine and they cost next to nothing. Papa lifts me up so that I can press a coin into the slot. My stomach tingles as it drops and the machine spits out a printed ticket. On the ticket you can read the time, the date and how long we're able to occupy a space on the street. That's all. A pleasant feeling, the excitement of getting a piece of paper from a machine. I think we're stealing a parking space from someone.

I go to the swings. Swing to and fro, to and fro, long hair flying, my stomach fluttering. Sticky ice-cream fingers grip iron chains. In the corner of my eye a bird, a cloud, Papa reading the newspaper. I can sit here for hours.

On the way home a seagull poops right on the top of my head. I rub the buildings with my shoulder, walking tight behind Papa. Will he help me to wash it out when we get home? Maybe we'll rinse my hair in the kitchen sink; maybe we'll just wipe it off with a paper towel.

2016

It's November, early morning, and I've just packed Natasha off to daycare. The first freeze laid a fragile, overnight crust on all the puddles. I walk with quick steps across the pavements in Södermalm when Papa phones. His voice sounds happy; at the same time he's almost out of breath. He reads a letter out loud in broken Swedish, stuttering through each syllable.

'The Nobel Foundation ... requests the pleasure ... of the company of ... Mister Israel Young ... at the Prize Award Ceremony on the tenth of December at sixteen thirty ...'

He interrupts his reading, says he can't see if I'm invited too. I ask him to read a little slower. He reads it again, carefully enunciating every word:

'... to be held in the Stockholm Concert Hall and the following banquet in the Stockholm City Hall ... No, there isn't anything in the letter about you!'

'If you turn it over ...'

'What?'

'Maybe there's something written on the back?'

He reads the same sentence again and again. Finally, he raises his voice, demanding to know what we should do, who we should call. He wants me to rush home and see if I also got a letter. I tell him that I can't do it right away. At the same time I'm thinking, *Well, well, let's see what happens.*

Perhaps I should call someone, maybe the woman from the Swedish Academy who asked me for Dylan's number. I thumb through my text messages searching for the one I sent her, hear Papa stumbling again:

'. . . requests the pleasure of the company of Mister Israel Young at the Prize Award Ceremony . . .'

He calls me again the next day and manages to read the whole letter word for word and in the right order. Now that he can breathe between sentences we are able to understand that he is expected to bring a companion.

That evening Papa is to have dinner at our place. I pick him up at the store.

'Did you bring the Nobel Prize invitation?' I ask as I help him into the car.

He says he doesn't remember. He might have left it at home, on the kitchen table. I make a U-turn, drive towards Papa's apartment in Fredhäll, knowing it's best that I find the invitation before it disappears. If it hasn't disappeared already.

I leave Papa sitting in the dark, in the car, while I hurry through the entrance to his building. Too impatient to wait for the lift, I run up five flights of stairs. The key slips into the lock. It's been a while since I was last here. The light in the hallway doesn't work and I make a mental note to get it fixed. How long has it been broken? Pictures of me and the children are on the fridge that he's pushed out into the hallway. A lone painting on his bedroom wall, a dusty alarm clock on the bedside table, a few potted plants in the window. A potato has been placed inside a flowerpot, above which a swarm of fruit flies dances.

In thirty seconds I've gone through his one room and the kitchen. I should help him put up some more paintings; it's too bare here. He doesn't really live here; the apartment is just a thing he's forced to have. His life is in the store.

The invitation, in a small bright white envelope, lays on the kitchen table that doubles as his desk. Even wiped, the table has a sticky, film-like veneer that's impervious to scrubbing. On the front of the envelope with fat black letters he's written '10 December'. Carefully, I slip it into my coat pocket. I really should go back to Papa, but something smells. Strongly. I check the bed, lift the blanket stretched neatly over his mattress. Someone from home services must have made it. The blue sheet underneath is wrinkled, littered with flakes of dead skin, like a layer of gravel. I don't have time to deal with it. Another mental note: *Remind home services that they have to make him use the moisturizer. They have to shake out his sheets. Every day!* A hard punch to my stomach. I need to come here more often, help him more. What is that smell?

When I open the bathroom door the stink hits me full force. I turn the light on. Could it be dirty clothes in the laundry basket? The toilet lid is open. The bowl is clogged. I try flushing several times. I fill a vase with water from the kitchen. Papa's waiting in the car; soon he'll trudge upstairs, probably worried that I can't find the letter. He'll leave the car unlocked. My kids are home waiting for supper. Why do I carry the responsibility for all of this by myself?

I pour vase after vase of water over what's in the toilet. How long has it been clogged? One day, two days . . . Still impossible to flush. Only one thing left to do. I get the ugliest kitchen knife I can find. The absurdity of the situation strikes me. Here I am, coat on, with that elegant invitation tucked away in my pocket, cutting what needs to be cut. No gloves. Just do it. I flush again. It works. Quickly I stuff the knife into a rubbish bag, tie it and run down the stairs. I hear the swishing sound as the bag falls down the rubbish chute.

Outside it's drizzling, as if the weather can't decide between autumn or winter. I call Lasse and explain why we're late. If he'd had to do what I just did he would have thrown up. I'm sure of it. Papa is a dark silhouette in the passenger seat. He's relieved when he sees me climbing into the car, can't remember that there was ever a problem. I believe he feels sorry for me when I describe what I just went through.

We drive home and he talks the whole way about how healthy and strong he is, how he walks every day for hours:

'Nobody can beat me!'

And yeah, he's right. Eighty-eight years old and the man is as healthy as an ox.

1981

If you are on the ground floor at Skeppsholmsgården it always smells of tar. That's because during the daytime they teach boat building here. Thick ropes coil on the plank floor. I pretend that they're snakes. A narrow wooden staircase leads to a trap door in the ceiling. When I push it open, I can see Papa's feet and everyone up there dancing. He's shouting, calling out the steps. On the dance floor his word is law.

'ONE, TWO, THREE, FOUR!'

I go upstairs and sit in a chair, dangling my feet, watching Papa teach square dance. He stomps the rhythm with his feet and hollers. Papa's square-dance orchestra, the Steamboat Entertainers, are all whooping, howling. The floor underneath them quakes. Papa steps in, pulls and pushes the beginners. The fiddler's stomach tries to escape his trousers, sweat pours, strings burst, his moustache is huge and he always wears braces. There's another musician with a moustache too; he sings with a tiny nasal voice. Then there's a woman playing banjo, her hair always tied up in a bandana. I've known them all since I was a baby.

'Back to BAAAAACK!'

One of the dancers does some steps wrong and Papa pulls him roughly, puts him where he's supposed to be, and mutters:

'Schmuck and fucking idiot!'

I look the other way. Hear the fiddler shout:

'For fuck's sake, Izzy, calm down!'

The instruments pound again. I'm on the floor now, dancing with my daddy.

'SASHAY DOWN!'

No one can dance like me and him.

The others stand in two long lines, clapping, howling, whistling. We gallop right down the middle. I'm tiny, half as tall as all the others, but I have the rhythm. I fly, hair swinging. My hands have a steady grip on Papa's.

'Left hand around, right hand around. CHAAAANGE PARTNERS!'

He is focused, needs to show all the steps, but between our hands, his great, strong fists and my sturdy light ones, music flows.

During the break I sit in the fiddler's lap, clowning around, joking, playing. I eat a sandwich. His cheeks are fat, hands enormous, he smells of chewing tobacco. He picks up two spoons, lets them gallop like wild horses on knees, tabletops and my shoulders. I can't stop laughing. The break is over and the Steamboat Entertainers take their positions again. I lie down, press my cheek against the floor and rest. The floor is creaking.

I'm always there. Of course. Both when he teaches dance and when he has concerts, even if it's late at night. Mostly I just hang around, sneaking in the corners, playing, finding other rooms, rooms that are mine. I know how to sell tickets, I know how to make friends with the people who work the different venues. I know how to wait and I know how to sleep on Papa's jacket behind the loudspeakers. His journal is in one breast pocket and his pen is in the other.

It's late and the dance class is finished. Papa pulls out a wad of money and splits it equally with the musicians. I ride on his shoulders, all the way home to Södermalm. The moon shines. On us. On the bridge and on all the windows of the palace across the water.

2016

I've picked up Papa at the store. We cross streets, move along pavements on our way to the doctor's. I have a cold and don't really have the energy to go with him. I ask how it went the day before, with the guys that are making a documentary about him. He has no idea what I'm talking about, doesn't remember that he spent the whole of yesterday afternoon with them. He laughs and says:

'They don't mean anything to me anyway. Everybody wants a piece of me!'

He dodges the question, like he's done so many times this past year, and that's just as well. He doesn't remember anything at all from this morning either. Despite that, he is still so totally himself. Just like he's always been, curious and eager as a child. He still stops several times to point at something interesting he has just noticed. It takes a hundred years to walk 10 metres. The knitted hat he's wearing is neon yellow and his hands are red from cold.

It's our first visit to this clinic. Quiet, like a library. We both admire the wood panelling in the lift and the stone

floors. In the waiting room, sitting side by side on a sofa
with flowery cushions, we share a tangerine. The disinfect-
ant smell moves aside for the smell of the citrus. Papa wants
me to have more pieces than him as I haven't had time for
lunch yet. We leaf through magazines, he laughs, points at
headlines on the cover of a gossip rag:

'It's too complicated!'

The clock ticks. The doctor is late. It doesn't matter
where we go, the doctor is always late. I think that I could
maybe lean against Papa, close my eyes for a minute or
so. I move closer, let my head fall to one side, my cheek
against his shoulder. I jerk. His shoulder's hard now. When
did that happen? I lift my head, shocked, deprived of my
papa's shoulder.

The protests begin as soon as we step into the examin-
ation room. Papa doesn't understand why he needs a
check-up. He points to the doctor but looks at me, smiling
conspiratorially and whispering that it's all just a waste
of time. I get worried that this new doctor will take it
personally. He isn't laughing with us, not the way women
physicians usually do when they see us. This doctor wants to
ask direct questions. I stay in the background, answer when
Papa doesn't remember or doesn't understand. The doctor
asks him to remove his shirt. Papa flinches at the touch of
the cold stethoscope, gets goose bumps. I hold out his shirt.

'Shall I put it over your shoulders?'

'No.'

I'm sitting behind him, slightly to one side. I see the

shoulder I just tried to lean against, bones that are pushing against the skin. He's strong and thin at the same time. A small round stomach, hairy in places. Skin soft. Still Papa's skin, even if his shoulder isn't what it once was.

In bad English and with a serious demeanour, the doctor proclaims that everything is as it should be. Papa is elated, punches the air with abandon:

'I told you! Now you have to admit it, I'm really strong!'

The doctor still isn't laughing, but the receptionist does when Papa tells her that this was the best clinic he's ever visited.

'I'll be back in a couple of years! I only came here today because my daughter made me.'

2016

Light November drizzle hits the store windows. A concert is about to begin. Lasse has the children tonight. The two women who are sharing the bill are warming up in the cellar. There's a steep wooden staircase right behind the kitchenette leading downstairs. The sound of their harmonica and guitars reaches me and Papa. We arrange the chairs, a mix of old French café chairs in dark wood and folding chairs from IKEA, for the evening's audience. From the outside, the store looks like someone's living room; warm, inviting. Attached to the bookshelves are two lights fitted with extra-strong bulbs, pointed towards the space where the musicians will soon be standing. There is no real stage. Microphones and amplifiers have long since been banned. 'If you have something to say, we'll hear it', is Papa's motto.

The computer starts beeping. It's Papa's brother Oscar on Skype from the USA. Papa hurries to the corner desk to answer and just as swiftly the bickering begins. It's their thing. They call every other day to argue, to squabble bitterly in New York accents. They can't resist it.

Today Oscar is eating a bowl of cornflakes, his bull-dog pants in the background. He pulls the dog into the picture:

'Say hi to Max!'

Papa couldn't care less, he complains, says he has a concert in half an hour:

'Can't you see I'm busy?'

He points at the chairs in rows and the evening's first customer walking in through the door. The man has obviously never been here before because he's holding out a credit card. Papa yells that he must be joking, this place is 'cash only', but there is an ATM around the corner where the guy can take out money.

'I'll save a seat for you!'

The man exits. Oscar persists; he wants to show a box of old stuff he just bought on eBay. He holds up a theatre programme from the forties, wonders if Papa remembers when they were kids and used to go to the Yiddish theatre on the Lower East Side. Papa throws up his arms and sits down in front of the computer:

'Of course!'

The brothers' eyes become teary. They look like twins, same balding heads, same noses, same huge, wide hands. Even their voices sound alike. Papa laughs and reminds Oscar how they would, after the Sunday matinée, walk over to the Chinese restaurant where their mother worked. He loved the crispy duck. Oscar grins and says:

'Yeah, that was the only time you ever shut your mouth.

When you were eating!' He imitates how Daddy used to chomp and greedily lick his fingers.

'I was always the best eater', is Papa's immediate reply.

The musicians stomp up from the cellar with their instruments. One of them has a pierced eyebrow and a ring in her lip. A Venus symbol dangles from her ear and red tangled hair sprouts from under her captain's cap. A harmonica holder circles her neck. Her gaze is so intense that I can't tell if she's dangerous or maybe just one of those few grown-up people in whom the child still lives. The other woman is older. She has short pageboy hair, a fringe falling over rounded glasses, a striped shirt and a cap neatly pulled down over her brow. She is short and grouchy, holds her guitar in a firm grip. Both wave to Oscar. Papa stands and says he has to go.

'Just a minute!' shouts Oscar.

Papa groans but is soon lost again in a haze of nostalgia; this time it's his mother's chicken soup, simply seasoned with salt and pepper. How they sucked the drumsticks while their mother worried that Papa would break his teeth stubbornly trying to crush the chicken bone into crumbs.

One of Papa's friends, George, comes in. He's around eighty, one hand shaking from Parkinson's. His eyes though, they're perky. In the corner of his mouth he always has a wry joke ready. You often see him and Papa walking together, two sun hats bobbing side by side in the middle of the coldest winter. They go to concerts together; Papa gets the free tickets and George finds their way to the venues. George doffs his hat:

'Oh, is it your brother? Are you friends today?'

Oscar's wife pops into the frame now, waving, surprised to see a crowd looking back at her. We blow heartfelt kisses to one another as she deposits a bagel and the *New York Times* in front of Oscar. He sees a headline referring to the Israeli–Palestinian conflict and can't help reading it out loud. Seconds later, the brothers are bitter enemies. Words like 'schmuck' and 'fucking fascist' fly like bullets. Papa screams he needs to work, but allows Oscar to stay online and watch the concert.

Oscar mumbles, spreading cream cheese on his bagel. Max, the bulldog, licks the screen. Papa pushes chairs aside on his way to the door where guests stand waiting to buy a ticket. He mutters that he can't believe what a dope his brother is and says he can't stand watching him stuffing his face and talking bullshit with his mouth full.

The audience streams through the door holding the tiny ticket Papa gives them, hanging wet coats on the backs of chairs, warming up with cheap wine from plastic cups. Oscar watches the whole concert, he pets his dog, takes off and puts on his Yankees cap. He doesn't walk well these days so when the dog needs exercise he puts him on the treadmill. The dog runs, panting, looking with admiration at his master.

The women hit the guitar strings hard or pluck them softly. The wild one sings a rough-voiced song about her father. I look at my papa. He guards the door, seated on the deep marble ledge in the store's front window. He listens to the song, drumming the rhythm with his fingers against his knees. The windows are steamy from condensation.

Dad said, here you get a ship
which can sail on land and at sea
I tugged my little lip
when I understood that he had to leave

He was going to a distant land
the ship of air he put in my hand
and said fill it now with all your years
one day you'll conquer these fears

Papa looks up and sees me watching him. He smiles and waves. Occasionally he'll walk over to the computer and turn it slightly so that Oscar can see the show from different angles. He whispers:

'Isn't this a great concert?'

Oscar nods ambiguously, but looks happy.

When the evening is over, some of the audience stay behind to help put away chairs and tables. There are also one or two who've had more than their fair share of the wine. Papa is tired, more than usual. He blows a goodbye kiss to his brother. Oscar, happy, waves back and is quick to add:

'I'll call you tomorrow. I have more stuff I want to show you.'

'Come on, give me a break,' Papa whines.

He pats the screen. Oscar pats it back. They disconnect and for the next few hours the distance between them is re-established.

1981

I'm at a Dylan concert with Papa. We sit on the third row because Dylan's office has given us free tickets. As soon as the man on stage starts, his singing cuts through my body; I stand up:

'Papa, I want to go home.'

He wants to stay, grasps my forearm firmly and whispers. I twist myself free and take determined steps towards the aisle. He follows. Of course, he's forced to. Someone points, wide-eyed, saying, 'Look! Izzy Young is walking out!' I press my hands over my ears to stop the music. Run up a million stairs. When I get to the entrance, the place where we just came in, Papa grabs hold of me and falls to his knees, looks me right in the eyes:

'You have to understand. We can't leave now. Please . . .'

I understand that it's important. In some way that man on the stage is a friend of Papa's. So I wait, crying soundlessly on Papa's shoulders. Another two long numbers. Then we go.

The next day we're in the store. I'm drawing princesses in

my diary and Papa is helping me write what they're saying. Mostly it's about princes and about love. A man opens the door and pops his head in:

'Hey, Izzy, did you get to meet Dylan after the concert?'

Papa answers 'Schmuck' and continues filling in speech balloons.

In the park, later, the same thing happens. Some guy comes up to Papa and asks if he got to meet Dylan. It goes on that way the whole day. In the grocery store, walking down the street, in our stairwell. I don't know if we should feel ashamed. Should Papa be ashamed? Should I, because Papa didn't get to meet Dylan this time either? Every time Dylan plays a concert in Stockholm people smile strangely and keep asking that same question. Are they mocking or are they genuinely interested? Some of them don't even believe that Papa knows that guy Bob Dylan.

2016

There's a charming, old-fashioned bookstore on the hilly part of Götgatan. It has ladders leaning against shelves, rising all the way up to the ceiling. A cold wind blows through the open door as I slip inside. I'm looking for a copy of Bob Dylan's autobiography. I really should have read it years ago, but now, weeks before the Nobel Prize Banquet, I feel like I have to. There was a lot of talk about the book when it came out, partly because there was a section where Dylan wrote about Papa. He was also asked to read the introduction to the audiobook when it was released in Sweden. On a shelf in his store he has copies in several languages. A box full of books was sent over from Dylan's office. I can't remember being asked if I wanted one.

The book came out over ten years ago, so I called the bookstore in advance to make sure they had a copy. Now I'm searching for it, dark shelf by dark shelf. I don't know why, but I feel too embarrassed to ask for it. I don't want anyone to see me buying it. Did I decide somehow that Dylan shouldn't be important to me?

Finally, I find the book obscured by one of the ladders. I approach the cash register with the book stuck between two volumes of poetry. When I pay I look the other way, pull my hat low so my eyes are hidden. I smell wood and paper, see winter-clad literature buffs scanning book covers. I imagine that it looked a bit like this in Papa's store in New York, or maybe in places where he bought books. The woman at the cash register smiles and I slip the autobiography into a clear plastic bag I am given.

I walk to a park and sit down on one of the benches. It's so cold today that there aren't any children playing. There are only statues of bears staring at me when I open the first page. I leaf through the book, find the pages about Papa. I sink into Dylan's language. What he writes about Daddy's store in New York sounds beautiful. Intuitively I know that what he writes is true. Dylan describes Papa's place as a chapel the size of a shoebox with a little stove and walls covered with old, bent-up photographs of musicians. Papa's voice like a bulldozer and folk music was like shining gold for him, same as it was for Dylan. He recalls that Papa was always being hounded by people demanding money, but that it didn't seem to concern him. On the other hand, Papa is described as easily irritated and never afraid to say what he was thinking. Dylan doesn't seem to fully comprehend all that Papa was battling. I smile, recognize my father. The dampness of the bench has seeped through my jeans. I stand, walk swiftly homewards with the book tucked back into the clear plastic bag.

2010

Nikolai is young and still lets me hold his hand. I've just picked him up from school and we're strolling home along the steep paths in Vitabergsparken. He is telling me about which letters he learned to write today. A friend of Papa's telephones from the store. His voice cracks and he's speaking faster than he normally does.

'Something just happened to Izzy, but he's okay now.'

He describes how Papa sat frozen in front of the computer with a finger pressing one of the keys making long lines of a single letter: FFFFFFFFFFFFFFFFFFFFFFFFF FFFFFFFFFFFFFFFFFFFFFFFFFFFFFFFFFFFFFFFFFF FFFFFFFFFFFFFFFFFFFFFFFFFFFFFFFFFFFFFFFFFFF FFFFFFFFFFFFFFFFFFFFF

Papa doesn't recall anything of what happened and when the friend tried to explain, Papa got angry and started shouting. The man's voice is out of breath, though he tries to sound calm.

'I'm sure it's nothing serious. He's probably eaten too

many sweets. It might be a sugar shock? It happens to people with diabetes, even if they have the mild type . . .'

It happens again.

Papa and I are walking along a cobblestoned street by Mariaberget. Suddenly he stops midstep. A statue. Twenty seconds later it is over. He is back, picking up the conversation exactly where it ended. He doesn't believe me when I tell him what just happened.

A few months later we travel to Łódź, the industrial town where both of Papa's parents were born. Neither Papa nor I had ever been to Poland and he has seldom spoken about his parents' homeland. I only know that they moved before the Second World War and that my grandfather, when he was young, sold clothes to soldiers stationed at the German border.

I had reserved rooms at an expensive, art-deco hotel. The floor is polished, dried roses are arranged over fireplaces, antique bicycles hang on walls. The sun beats down on pavements and during the daytime the temperature reaches thirty degrees. Papa walks slowly but with purpose. Up one street, down the next. Looking for Jewish bakeries that resemble the one his parents had. He wants to find real challah, a light, plaited loaf covered with poppy seeds. My grandpa was often asked to bake these, especially for Jewish holidays. Sometimes they could be nearly three metres long and in order to bake them perfectly, each strand in the plait needed to have its own specific thickness.

Papa eavesdrops on people talking in the street; he can only understand a few words. When he was a child his parents spoke Yiddish while he and his brother answered in English. For the first time he now understands that some of what he thought was Yiddish was actually Polish. We talk in much the same way, Papa and I. He speaks English and I answer him most of the time in Swedish.

We ride trams, stop for coffees, sample *pirogi*, visit churches, glare at pigeons and lick ice creams. We walk and walk, mile after mile, under the hot sun. Both of us want him to be as strong as always.

We take a day trip into Warsaw and for the first time in my life somebody spits at us. Because Papa is a Jew. Because you can see that he is. That we are? It happens just as we come out of a museum about the Holocaust. Just before, we'd stared at an empty marmalade jar in a display. The text underneath explained how this very jar of preserve saved a family of four from starvation. It was all they had to eat for a whole week while they stayed hidden, waiting to be smuggled out of the country. We read about the deportations to Auschwitz, saw a film showing the emaciated bodies of the dead stacked high in piles.

When we leave the darkness of the museum, we inhale fresh air and are dazzled by the white sun. We walk, dazed, to the pedestrian crossing and stand waiting for the light to change. Then it happens. Swiftly and suddenly, too fast for me to register. I just see the man pass, mutter, continue walking. He's not even in a hurry. A white, bubbly stream of spittle glides slowly down the breast of Papa's shirt. With a green leaf from a shrub I wipe it off. Neither of us says a word. We walk, hand in hand, over streets that still have marks from the boundary of the ghetto where almost half a million Jews were imprisoned.

Back in Łódź again, the other thing happens. Twice. Papa freezes like a statue, stares at nothing. Thirty-mile-long seconds. As if the entire city holds its breath. When life returns to his eyes he has absolutely no recollection that anything has happened. He doesn't want to believe me, but he doesn't mind sitting down to rest. In the evening, it happens again. Previously it had been months between the incidents; now it's happened twice in the same twenty-four hours. While Papa waits on a bench, I rush off to the nearest tourist shop to buy a sun hat.

And that's not the end of it.

When we get back to the hotel, he doesn't recognize the entrance. He doesn't believe me when I say that we've arrived. Once inside the lobby he remembers and jokes with the porter, but he doesn't remember which room he's staying in. He laughs.

I become efficient. Silent. A look of understanding passes between me and the porter. I open Papa's door with the ancient key and lead him inside. From now on I can't leave him alone, not even for a second. I hide in the romantic bathroom, steady myself against the wash basin and try to catch my breath. I stare at the woman in the mirror. She who is me, she that looks so strange with a large nose and an ugly new haircut. I am in the wrong country and in the wrong place if the worst thing of all is to happen.

From now on I always carry a bottle of water with me. I wet his hat, I make sure we always sit in the shade. I don't let him out of my sight, not even for a minute. If I need to buy something I run as fast as I can. If I'm standing in a queue and he's sitting, waiting on a bench, I'm always looking in his direction. Between the walks and all the ice creams I lay on the bed, beneath its silk canopy. I gasp for air, choking on the sugary odour of scented candles and roses. I call my friend who is a nurse. She gives me advice and tells me that we can wait until we're home in a couple of days before we need to go to the hospital.

On our last night we go to a rock concert. Juliette Lewis. It's outside a cinema museum and the evening is cool. Juliette's shoulders are a riot of feathers and she moves ecstatically across the stage. I loosen my grip, leaving Papa at the back of the crowd. He leans against a loudspeaker, has promised that he won't move. I'm standing in the front but I look back at him constantly. He's listening, watching, making notes in his journal. Just as he's always done. We delight in the music, apart, but still together.

In the middle of the night, in a lurching tram, we ride back to the hotel. Side by side, both of us in childish appreciation of the night's music.

Straight away on landing in Stockholm I take him to the hospital's emergency department. Papa thinks I'm being ridiculous, but he goes along with it. We sit in the waiting room for hours, suitcases standing next to our chairs. The doctor calls it 'petit mal', a mild form of epilepsy, nothing dangerous. There is also a 'malignant glioma' in Papa's brain. Neither is a cause for concern as they've come so late in life. The episode with his memory could possibly be a symptom of fatigue. I, the daughter, that drove the old mule too hard.

1982

I love our apartment at Kocksgatan. It's filled with sunshine, and it's four metres up to the ceilings. I live one week here and one week with my mother. Weekends are best because then I don't have to go to school. We have three rooms and in the kitchen there's a pantry with an extra little hatch on the top. If you climb up on the top of the fridge and crawl through the hatch you get into a passage that leads the entire way to the living room. Papa put a mattress and some cushions in the passage so that I can play there.

I always go barefoot when I'm home. Sometimes I sit on a chair or a sofa and brush the soles of my feet with my hands. Then you can hear crumbs fall from them, like fine gravel. They make a tiny pile on the floor. I let them stay there.

Our forks are heavy and made with real silver. They taste like metal. In the space between each tine there's a crust of dried, brown gunge. I scrape away at it with my knife before we eat. It's like cleaning under your fingernails. But I'm almost never sick. Neither is Daddy. We're healthier than most.

We live in a kind of commune that's not a commune. It's two apartments attached by a simple door between them. We each have our own kitchen, but they have the shower. A girl lives on the other side and we pretend she's my little sister. She's five and I'm eight. When she was a baby they let me change her nappy. We scamper back and forth, between the two apartments. We never knock. Suddenly she's in our place or I'm in hers.

In the evening, if no one on the other side is home, Papa says that I can go in there. I open the door and sneak in, tiptoe past their bed and things. Blue light enters from the street lamps that sway outside the windows. Their side smells like cigars because my little sister's dad smokes them. He even smokes in the car.

You only need to go through one room to reach their living room. To the TV. It stands beside the fireplace. I press ON and turn the volume low so nobody in the hallway outside can hear it. I switch back and forth between channel one and channel two. Lying on my stomach, I press myself against the floor; it tingles nicely between my legs, but I can't make any sounds. I need to hear if they're coming. At the slightest sound from the stairs my heart jumps and I'm on my feet, running through the door into ours.

In our apartment, warmed by the sun, I draw princesses on the walls. I'm allowed to. It takes time. The dress, the hair, the crown. When I wake up in the morning they smile at me. Sun is shining on their faces because we don't have curtains.

In the living room Papa built a loft bed made of wood. It reaches almost all the way up to the ceiling. It's so high that I can still sit on Papa's shoulders under it without hitting my head. He hung a swing underneath. I swing as much as I like and listen to the radio. The higher I swing the louder the boards underneath the mattress groan. From up in the bed I get dizzy when I look down at the sofa. I climb up and hop down, climb up and hop down, hair flying, and I lip-sync to songs on the radio.

I always sleep up there, next to Daddy. I like to lie on my back and drum my feet against the cool plaster ceiling. At night I watch the headlights from passing cars sweep across the walls. With my hands, I can almost catch the shadows. Papa sleeps on the outside; a rickety railing keeps him from falling. I sometimes lie at the foot of the bed with my head hanging over. I can only look down for a few seconds before I feel dizzy. We sleep like that, tight together, until Mama decides that we shouldn't anymore. Even though she doesn't live here. She says that I am too big now.

My room is full of teddy bears. I have a bed and a dressing table with a mirror and some hairbrushes. There are posters and pictures on the wall. Papa always sticks the drawing pin right through the picture when he helps me hang them up. Tiny striped insects crawl on the carpet and sometimes on my teddies. I hardly ever play in there; I prefer playing in the living room or at my sister's next door.

2011

Patti Smith sings wide-mouthed into the microphone. She is playing at Cirkus, a large venue in Stockholm, and her dark voice vibrates through the arena. Her hands draw magic symbols in the air and her hair flies wild around her face as her feet stomp a heavy-booted tempo on the stage floor. She tips the microphone stand, leans it up against her body. Sweat pours off her. I want to be her, and I never want her to stop. Papa and I sit as if we are in a trance.

I have no memory of ever having met her in person, but under the sink in Papa's store are some old reel-to-reel tapes. On one of them a young Patti Smith reads poetry on a radio show Papa had in New York. The tape box is square and has dents in it. But the year 1966 is visible in neat cursive script on the coffee-stained cover. We found the pile of recordings by accident; they stood behind some old flowerpots that we were about to throw out. We played the reel-to-reel at a friend's recording studio. Patti's young, soft voice filled the room. Sombrely, she recalled how she'd always been a tomboy and thought that being a girl was a drag. The boys, they were the cool ones. She had realized only recently that being a girl was neat, but she didn't really know how to be one. She said: 'And I still haven't learned how to sport a cocktail dress, but by writing about girls, you know, just writing about myself, I'm sort of getting more the feel of it.' Then she read a couple of 'girl poems'. Fragile and careful. Something completely different to that force of nature blasting from the stage in front of us. Papa's voice is also preserved on that tape; he introduced her before she began reading, said that Patti would perform at the Folklore Center that same evening. His voice, dark and gravelly, still had a touch of youth in it. Different, but I recognized it without any doubt.

Patti finally seems to decide that the concert is over, that we've had all that we can take. She releases her hold on us, struts sassily from the stage. The ceiling lights fade up, dispelling the magic. The crowd, dazed, begins to stand. Papa and I stumble backstage.

On stage her energy seemed inexhaustible, but here, backstage, she is grey and pallid. Worn. It's awkward between Papa and Patti, none of the flow of the heartfelt greetings that are usually part of our visits to Papa's friends backstage. Maybe she's tired after the concert; maybe she doesn't have the energy for us. Too shy to look at her directly, I steal glimpses of her profile in the dressing-room mirror. She's tough-looking in her black suit jacket and white shirt sleeves that cover her hands.

In front of the mirror a table is crowded with dishes, filled with nuts, kiwi and dried papaya, only healthy things. We dig into them in silence. Even Papa seems at a loss to know what to do or say. I'm just about to suggest a retreat when Patti's guitarist, Lenny Kaye, walks through the door. With him there's no hesitation, he loves Papa and they hug several times. Laughter fills the dressing room while Patti moves restlessly about, staring at the floor.

We're leaving when she says she can't find her glasses. She's searching and searching, noticeably stressed. I start looking too. Finally I crawl under the bed in her dressing room. There is dust on the floor and my jacket gets dirty, but in the corner I find them. Patti's face lights up when I slide out holding her glasses.

As we're leaving, she shouts out to me in the hallway:

'You saved my life; I can't read without my glasses!'

Papa and I catch the ferry back to Södermalm. The sea smells. The baby-blue sky is flecked with pink. Our eyes fall on the dome of Katarina Church and the bridges over the locks at Slussen. Waves beat the side of the ferry and Papa says:

'You know, even when she was young, I was scared to death of her. She was a kid, but such a damn revolutionary force!'

That same year I'm in New York, walking in the Village. I sit on a bench in Washington Square Park, enjoying the spring sunshine, listening to some guys singing a cappella. Their groove is so wonderful that I could almost cry. I close my eyes, listen to their deep voices.

In the early sixties the New York City authorities decided that live music should be banned from the park. Enraged, Papa organized a demonstration. In a black-and-white film of the event, I watch him putting up signs in the store window, calling for a protest. Hundreds of musicians descend on the park, armed with instruments. Papa stands high up on the fountain and his narrow black tie flies in the wind as his voice booms across the square. The thick, horn-rimmed glasses strengthen his air of determination as he starts a sing-along and gets everyone to join him. His mouth is wide open when he sings and he doesn't need a megaphone to be heard in the chaos that occurs when the police cars enter the park.

Papa has told me that he'd counted on the police not having the heart to attack citizens singing children's songs. Unfortunately, he had miscalculated. Police batter protestors, drag them into waiting paddy wagons. High up on the fountain, Papa is never in any danger. I even see my grandmother in the film, her chalk-white hair freshly curled. She shields her breast with her handbag. The demonstration, later called the 'Beatnik Riot', was a success. Live music is still allowed in the park today. The film is called *Sunday* and you can view it on YouTube. I watch it sometimes, a small piece of history.

Eyes closed, fingers snapping, the men near my bench go on twining their harmonies. They seem joyful, lost in concentration. I imagine them meeting here every day. Red squirrels scamper under my feet and across the park.

By the arch, someone is pushing a piano. The minute he has it where he wants it he sits and begins playing Mozart. At the same time a woman is setting up a PA system by the fountain. Her determined expression suggests that she's planning to hold a fiery speech.

Somehow, I can't stop thinking that everything going on here is partly because of Papa. Perhaps he'll be remembered in the future with a golden plaque on one of these park benches. That would be beautiful.

I want to see where Papa's old store in the Village used to be, so I wander through the nearby streets and alleyways. I know that it was here in the Village, but I don't remember the exact address. It's three in the afternoon in New York, not too late to phone home. A truck thunders by just as Papa answers. He has a hard time hearing what I say. Furthermore, Papa, who has always known the address by heart, can't bring it to mind now.

'It's just because it's late,' he says, in an attempt to brush it off.

I'm frustrated. And deep inside I feel a sadness; I don't want to acknowledge the warning signs heralding old age. Once we've hung up I step into the first guitar store I see and ask if they might possibly know where the Folklore Center used to be. I'm immediately given the street name and number.

Bright sun paints the facade of the building which once upon a time was the epicentre of the folklore revival. As I've understood it, it was here that my mother and father met for the first time in 1968. She came from France, was in her early twenties. Papa must have been around forty. The story goes that she tried to bargain her way into one of Papa's concerts. It riled him, but all the same they ended up taking a walk together after the concert, looking at the stars sparkling high up over the Brooklyn Bridge. They discussed poetry and books, shared the same curiosity about everything that was happening on every street corner.

In the end they fell in love, ate duck in Chinatown and started broadcasting a radio programme together. Mama studied art and moved in with Papa in the loft above his store. The loft, by all reports, was fabulous, though horribly cold in winter. Occasionally, and illegally, they harboured people evading the Vietnam draft. They attended meetings and printed flyers. They worked with the Washington Square Methodist Church, sharing with them a commitment to the anti-war movement, and also collaborating when Papa needed a bigger venue for concerts. They lived above the store for four years. Musicians looking for a gig at Papa's would audition upstairs in their apartment.

But sometime in the early 1970s Papa began to lose confidence, both in the country and in the recording industry. He felt that all the musicians were becoming too commercial and that Greenwich Village had turned into a tourist trap. He wanted to move to Sweden, to a life where he would have time to write. Mama had become more and more involved in the women's movement, which in Sweden was growing in strength. In the end it was she who pried them loose.

I look at the storefront which once was Papa's; I see all the black-and-white photographs I've stored in my memory. Papa, standing with a group of cool-looking African American musicians all leaning cockily against the railing in front of the store holding their guitars. Papa and Allen Ginsberg, standing in a living room, arm in arm, totally naked. Papa's profile in the evening sun through the store window; he's young, broad-shouldered and bent over a typewriter surrounded by instruments, records and flyers.

It's a falafel place now. I stand in front of the door pacing back and forth. The old handrail is still there. But I was never there, back then. Then, when it was magical.

1982

It's the summer holidays and we're taking the train to Jokkmokk. My bag is packed with comic books and a Barbie for a journey that lasts a hundred hours.

In Jokkmokk Papa is teaching square dance. It's midnight sun, reindeer, folk music and market stalls. The blue-and-yellow flag flutters and a sea of fiddlers alternate between playing sometimes wild and sometimes beautiful. It sounds screechy but nice at the same time. It smells of coffee and hot dogs. Papa is everywhere, carrying a paper bag full of his own newsletters, *News from the Folklore Center*. Today he's counted ten new subscribers; he already has over three thousand. 'More information about folk music than you'll find anywhere else' is written on the top of the front page.

I lost a tooth. Jagged and crusted with blood, it rests in Papa's pocket. Musicians, in unison, beat the floor with their feet. I run my tongue over the gap where my tooth used to be. It's gross and tastes of blood. It doesn't hurt really, but still, it feels as if my cheek is pulsating.

Papa sits down with me on his lap in the front row. He

always wants to sit close so that he won't miss anything. Now everyone looks at the stage instead of nagging me about some tooth fairy. He holds his warm hand over my cheek and I sit, as if in a cave, between his arms. When a lonesome nyckelharpa plays a quiet note, a couple in traditional folk costumes begin to dance, Papa gets tears in his eyes and whispers:

'Now you understand why I moved to Sweden.'

'I think knee socks are ugly.'

It feels strange where my tooth used to be. Like a part of me is gone. Tears well up in my eyes too, because the music is so beautiful, because I lost my tooth and I'll never have it back again. Because I think maybe Papa will die soon. He was already forty-seven when I was born and he is much older than everybody else's fathers. I wipe my nose with a finger and rub it off on Papa's trousers.

2016

A November morning and my dance partner and I are dancing the tango in the store. We've been paired at a dance course and sometimes we meet to practise. He holds me tightly and we glide past the chairs that are lined up against one of the walls. People on their way to work stop and smile when they see us through the windows. Papa sits at his round marble table, listens to the music, leafs through papers, trying not to disturb us. Sometimes he licks a finger and rubs off coffee stains from the table. In a pause between songs he asks if we'll be performing soon. We aren't anywhere near performance level but appreciate that he likes our dance steps.

When we've danced ourselves tired, we sit down beside him. I rub his back. There is a bad smell, and the odour comes from Papa. Should I say something? The smell is so obvious that I place a hand on his knee and ask:

'Did you have an accident?'

He admits it, but only a small, small . . .

My dance partner excuses himself with a hug, his eyes

full of understanding. He promises Papa that next time he'll bring cake.

'I'll be back in a minute!' I call, and jump on my bicycle.

Avoiding snowdrifts, I head towards the main street to find some new underwear. It isn't easy; the streets around Mariatorget haven't attracted any of the big clothing stores. Finally, in a semi-exclusive men's store, I find underwear. I wonder if the salesperson, who must assume I'm buying a present for my boyfriend, thinks I'm stingy when I choose the cheapest ones they have. I also stop at the grocery store to buy a large pack of wet wipes.

Back in the store again I lock the front door and walk down the stairs to the cellar with Papa. He has a camp bed down there, CDs piled in wobbly stacks, a sink, cleaning supplies, some clothes and a dirty fridge. Thick pipes that traverse the ceiling gurgle when someone in the building flushes their toilet. And down here is where all the poetry is.

Among bookshelves filled with well-worn volumes, I help him remove his trousers. He's not agile anymore, has to put a hand on my head for balance as I pull his trousers over his feet. It wasn't a small accident. His briefs are full. I get them off and immediately stuff them into a plastic bag. Tying it tightly, trying to lock the stench inside. I find a pair of rubber gloves and dry his legs and bottom with wet wipes. He flinches from the cold but stands there with legs spread wide and lets me do it. I use nearly the whole packet. The most difficult part is cleaning beneath his testicles. Finally, it's good enough and we pull on the newly purchased underpants made from woven bamboo fibres. They are soft, have a wide elastic band at the waist, cost almost three hundred kronor.

'It feels good now,' he asserts.

I wonder how long it will be before these underpants also end up in the rubbish.

When we climb the stairs into the shop again we're met with winter sunlight shining through the enormous windows, highlighting dirty stains and dust deposits on the blue linoleum floor. I put on a CD of bluegrass music. The joyful sound of fingerpicking fills the store. A neighbour comes in and delivers the morning paper he's just finished reading. He brings it every day. Papa's day is beginning.

I kiss his unshaven cheeks, buckle on my helmet, put the plastic bag with the soiled clothes in my bike basket, wave and roll down the hill. Fresh air bites my cheeks. I look for a rubbish bin so I can dispose of the bag as soon as possible. For the moment I'm relieved of guilt. I have done everything I could.

It's over between me and my boyfriend. I'm twenty-seven
and I'm crying all the time. Not so much when I'm with
Papa, but he knows I've got it bad. Stockholm's pavements are caked with ice and my legs are as stiff as sticks.
Sometimes I find myself sitting on the metro or on a bus
without the slightest idea where I'm going. One day I stop
by the store to see Papa. He runs his thumb across the dark
circles under my eyes, then he stands and yanks out one of
the stubborn drawers in the counter, fiddles among scissors,
pens and rubber bands until he finds an envelope containing
pictures of me and my ex:

'Come here,' he says, and takes my hand.

No coats, we stand outside on the pavement. Silently Papa
lights a match and sets a photo on fire, then another and
then another. One at a time. Black ashes from a relationship flutter down on the chalk-white snow. When all the
photos lie in flakes on the ground he puts his arm around
my shoulders and kisses my brow. We step back into the
warmth of the store.

A few months later I'm still mostly going around in tears. A singer passes Papa's store window. I'm not there but Papa told me later that he rushed outside saying he'd like to interview the man for his newsletter. Sitting in a café, talking about music, the singer confides in Papa that his wife had just left him for someone else. She's an actress and he's now persecuted by her naked image, next to that of her new lover, plastered on theatre posters all around the city.

'That's nothing,' says Papa. 'You should see MY daughter, she's crying all the time!'

Somehow, he feels the need to claim that I'm worse off, that he has one up on the singer. Thirty minutes later he's holding two free tickets to the singer's upcoming show at Nalen.

We go. I'm exhausted and haven't even bothered with mascara. Still, I make sure we get our own table with a good view of the stage. I notice that the singer, sitting behind the grand piano, looks in my direction a few times. He's handsome, wears a black suit and a hat, is probably a few years older than I am, but his eyes are shining. Every now and then he wipes the sweat from his face. Some of his songs make me laugh, others make me sad. He's clever with words. His fingers dance over the keys of the piano, the strings of his electric guitar. How would those hands feel on me? Perhaps I should have put on some lipstick . . .

In my bag I have a free ticket to a play that I'm currently performing in. I whisper to Papa:

'Do you think I should give him a free ticket, as a way of thanking him for the concert?'

The answer comes in an instant:

'Do it!'

After the concert I walk to the stage and shake the singer's hand. He smiles and introduces himself as Lasse. I don't really know how it happened. But minutes later we're sitting side by side on the edge of the stage, our feet dangling, talking about odd characters in the crowd. His ears are pointed like an elf's and I notice that his thigh muscles stretch his suit trousers. You can tell that he is from Halland, in the south of Sweden; the accent is softer there than here in Stockholm. His voice is dark and friendly. We're slightly apart but it feels like we're sitting close. I'm bold enough to give him the ticket and our fingers briefly touch before I go back to Papa.

We're about to leave when I see him standing across the room in the middle of a circle of women. I laugh to myself and think, *Forget about that one*. A ladies' man is the last thing I need right now. I wave an awkward goodbye and see him jump to attention, hurrying over to me and Papa.

'Listen, after your play, could I invite you out for a glass of wine?'

His eyes meet mine, his voice quivers slightly.

The whole way to the metro station Papa is overjoyed; he's constantly pulling my arm, shouts that the concert was fantastic and that he was the one who got us tickets:

'You see! I know how to make you smile.'

Ice turns to drops melting from drainpipes and we don't need to close our coats anymore. Something is tingling. Although right now, I have no idea that this man, the one I just waved goodbye to, will be the one who I'll share my life and have two kids with.

1982

The latest film with the Jönsson Gang, who I love, will soon begin. I'm eight years old and Papa gives me my ticket before he waves and leaves the cinema. The usher tears the ticket and I rush to find a seat. I'm wearing patent-leather shoes and they tap nicely against the floor. There are only four or five others in the cinema. There's usually more. Maybe because it's beautiful weather outside. I choose a row where no one is sitting and sink down into the red velvet seat in the middle. It's quiet, but for the low whispers of the tiny audience. Papa couldn't afford to come with me. He'll pick me up afterwards, when the film is over. He'll be waiting in the foyer. I've been to the cinema by myself before, but then it was at the Victoria, the little local cinema around the corner from where we live. Papa always sits right outside and waits for me. Today he's going to go somewhere to drink coffee. This cinema is by Kungsträdgården, in the middle of the city.

I look at the curtain. The ticket between my fingers is getting thin from sweat, nearly transparent. Isn't the film starting soon? It's so quiet I can hear the air going in and out through my nose. My heart is pounding. Why aren't the trailers starting? Can I give the ticket back? If I run, will I catch up to Papa? But we looked at all the film advertisements in the paper, circled the ones that looked the best, chose the Jönsson Gang film and took the bus into the city so that I could see it . . .

The curtain opens, dividing in the middle. I lean back; finally the theme music I love is playing. But mostly I'm looking at the others in the audience or up at the ceiling. The light streaming from the projector cuts through the darkness. Small lights in the floor mark the aisle. There, all the way at the back, is the door. That's where you can go out.

On the screen, Sickan, one of the main characters, sits in a big box, puffing out his cheeks so that he looks like a baby. No one in the cinema is laughing. They sit like paper dolls; light is glancing off the back of their heads as if they were dead. I look down at the floor, counting each breath, trying to concentrate. I wonder if anyone saw that I am alone, that I don't have any sweets? I don't want to be here. Suddenly I'm running. My body does it for me. My seat shuts with a thump and my heels punch hard against the floor. I propel myself out of the building, out into the sun. White! White! White! There's the church! Kungsträdgården is right behind it!

Legs racing, hair flying, skirt fluttering. I'm galloping but still careful not to fall. I have to find Papa before the tears start, before he disappears. I slalom past gaudy flower beds and families eating ice creams. I don't give a shit about the park's lions or fountains. My shoes pound the gravel paths of summer which promise scraped knees if I tumble. He's got to be here! I know which café he likes. It's outside and has green chairs, close to a big street. I take my longest strides. I'm Katitzi, I'm Madicken, I'm Ronja the Robber's Daughter. I see green chairs, there in the distance, behind the fountain. THERE'S PAPA!

He's sipping coffee, reading a newspaper, the pages close to his eyes, his glasses pushed high up on his forehead. He squints; wisps of grey hair in the breeze tickle his bald spot. He doesn't see me, but I see him. I'll be there in a second. Soon I'll tell him exactly what happened, maybe taste a teaspoon of his coffee. He won't be mad, but when I plonk down across the table from him, breathless, I'll start to think about the price of the ticket, money that was used for nothing. Maybe he'll think the same thing. He looks surprised when he sees me, wonders what happened. With his thumb he wipes the worried wrinkle from my forehead.

2016

Three weeks left until the Nobel Prize celebrations and I still don't know what to wear. That problem aside, there's a bunch of other stuff I need to work out. I write everything down on a piece of paper.

- Dress

- Handbag (must be large enough to hold phone, rubber gloves and a plastic apron)

- Hair and make-up

- Tuxedo

- Patent-leather shoes

- Silk stockings

- Bow tie and braces

- Cummerbund

- Dress shirt

- Nappy for Papa

- Call and see if it's possible for us to sit next to each other at the banquet

- Book a taxi

- Decide when the documentary team can film

- Important! Papa needs to nap before the evening

For the tenth time in a row I go into the city on a dress hunt. I venture into an exclusive boutique even though I'm wearing a worn-out down coat. A saleswoman comes over and asks:

'What is it you're looking for exactly?'

I say that I'm looking for something grand, something that could match my father and be suitable for a Nobel Banquet.

'I want this evening to become a lifelong memory.' The woman understands completely:

'Hmm ... Unfortunately, I don't think you'll find anything special enough here. But there is a designer I think you'll like. Did you check out Ida Sjöstedt?'

With sweat running down my spine and my body smelling, I look up the designer's webpage on my phone. Among small thumbnail pictures displaying various creations, I see it: the gown of my dreams. Black tulle, black lace, discreetly embroidered flowers, and glitter. A subdued, romantic ball gown. It would be perfect. Still standing in the store, my hand shaking slightly, I type an enquiry.

I'm on the bus when the reply comes. Ida asks which of the dresses I liked the most and if I'd like to come in for a fitting this Friday.

A few days later I'm getting myself ready to visit her showroom. I want to appear important enough that she'll agree to dress me. I pull on a pair of new sheer tights, an elegant but not-too-fancy black dress and then the overcoat I otherwise seldom wear. I place my heels in a carefully chosen paper bag and drive to her atelier on Kungsholmen. I park a few streets away, not willing to risk her spotting my rusty, pea-green Volkswagen.

An assistant greets me and leads me into a large dressing room with walls painted pink, freshly cut flowers on a table next to a sofa.

'These are the dresses we thought might suit you,' she says, pointing to some clothes racks that stand two metres high. Each gown is so thick with bobbinet that just a couple of them fit on a rack. I see that my dream dress is among those chosen.

'Ida will be right with you.'

With a friendly smile the assistant turns and leaves me alone in the room. I try looking sophisticated, sit on the sofa, scan my phone pretending to read something important. Most of all I would like to walk right up to the dresses and touch them.

Ida walks in, cool and with purpose:

'Which one do you want to try first?'

I point, undress, happy to have chosen a nice bra and knickers without holes. I suck in my tummy. The gown sweeps around me as Ida and her assistant pull the creation over my bare shoulders. Their fingers touch the skin of my back. Bobbinet brushes over my thighs. I see myself in the mirror. In the same second as they pull the zip up, every childhood fantasy I'd ever nourished comes true. I see beauty, another me.

Ida and her assistant circle me, inspecting every aspect of the fit. Both are nodding and Ida says:

'It couldn't fit better, it's as if we'd sewn it to measure. Even your heels fit the fabric perfectly.'

We shake hands. The dress and a matching coat with a purple fake-fur collar get bundled into black bags marked VIP. I walk to the car with arms heavily laden. Carefully, I arrange the bags on the back seat. I had already, before driving across town, pushed the comic books and empty fruit-drink cartons on to the floor, covered the dirty seat with a freshly washed bed sheet. Nothing should foul Ida Sjöstedt's creations.

Our apartment is filled with that peculiar silence that only exists when no children are home, though the living room holds clues of their presence galore: a half-eaten sandwich on the piano, a toothbrush next to the television, a pile of Lego bricks on the carpet. With reverence I hang each item of clothing on a hanger in front of the bookshelf. I sit on Lasse's piano stool and gaze at the coat and gown. I hear the kitchen clock ticking and a car tooting in the street below our window. I am silent. The dress glitters black and full of secrets.

1982

Today is Saturday and Papa doesn't have any money. There's nothing under the carpet, in his trouser pockets or in his jacket. We'll manage, he says. We always do. If we go to Kungsträdgården and sit on a bench there, someone's bound to walk by and invite us home for lunch or give us some money. It's worked before. I like this park – the king's park. There's a playground there, bronze lions hot from the sun and a fountain where water spouts from the mouths of swans.

While we're getting ready to go, I sit down next to the stereo. Papa's plastic headphones cover my whole cheeks. It's never long before they're warm and sweaty. The edge of one of the earpieces is broken. I poke my finger in, feel the soft, yellow foam. I'm listening to *The Jungle Book*. The record sleeve is in my lap and I look at the pictures: Mowgli and Baloo dancing in the jungle, Bagheera, with a surprised expression, falling out of a tree, Shere Khan and Kaa grooving. I know the whole record by heart. Baloo and Mowgli are like Papa and me, only more exciting. And in the end

Mowgli falls in love with a girl with long, dark hair and long eyelashes. I'm in love with Jon in second grade.

When I'm not listening to *The Jungle Book* I listen to another children's record.

'I'M JUST A TINY KITTEN!'

When that song starts, I sing, 'BOOM CHIKA, BOOM CHI-KA, BOOM BOOM BOOM, with the tiniest little MITTEN!'

I like sitting there, listening, spinning around in the swivelling chair. Thousands of tiny dust particles float in the air, like they're falling in slow motion.

At Kungsträdgården, next to the fountain, I crown the swans with leaves and flowers. When water comes from their mouths it looks like spit. Papa writes in his journal. I'm not worried; I've never had to go to bed hungry.

An hour later and still no one we know, but there is another fountain a couple of hundred metres away. People throw coins in it, believing their wishes might come true. If I take off my shoes and hitch up my skirt I can wade out into the cold water. I pick up shiny coins from the bottom and soon my wet hand is full. Papa reads the paper. My heavy haul is just enough to pay for a large tin of fish-balls in dill sauce and a few potatoes, or perhaps a slice of smoked salmon from the market stalls at Hötorget. Or maybe even two ice creams, the kind on a stick.

2016

Grouchy November. I'm sidestepping patches of ice and pedestrian traffic on the pavement, scurrying home with arms loaded heavy with groceries. The signals at each junction tick time while cars splash by. It's half-past five and it has long since been dark as winter is deepening. My pocket vibrates. With frozen fingers, grocery bags wrapped around my wrists, I manage to take out my phone. It's a withheld number. I answer.

'Hello?'

A velvety voice on the other end.

'Hi, I'm calling in regard to the Nobel Prize. Is this a good time to talk?'

Hollywood suddenly replaces the icy slush as my stomach stirs with anticipation.

'Yes, well, uhm … I'm just walking home, but I'll be there in a minute.'

He seems content with my answer and continues to speak slowly, taking care to articulate:

'Right. It seems our Nobel Prize winner in literature

sadly won't be accepting his prize in person this year.' He pauses. 'Therefore we're looking for someone who could read Bob Dylan's acceptance speech.'

Are they going to ask now if Papa can read the speech? The ceremony is two weeks away and the past few days it's all anyone I run into talks about. They give me a conspiratorial look and a little laugh:

'And whooooo do you think is going to read Dylan's speech . . .?'

They all think that I know something that I'm not allowed to tell, that Papa will have the honour. I wrestle the groceries up the stairs, have an impulse to blurt out in broad American, the way Papa usually does, 'Well why don't you just ask *me*!' But it's not appropriate to joke about the Nobel Prize, so I simply say:

'Okay.'

The man takes a deep breath and continues:

'So . . . we wanted to ask if you would consider reading Bob Dylan's acceptance speech at the banquet?'

I freeze, slam on the brakes. Just as I fantasized about doing a second ago, I blurt out:

'WHAT?! But it's Papa you should be asking! He's the one who knows Dylan. He's the one with that fantastic deep voice and the accent to match.'

The first round of a wrestling match playing out in my head immediately begins: *Would Papa manage it? Thank God I found such a fantastic gown! But what would Papa say if I got up to read the speech instead of him? And all his friends? I could get acting jobs in foreign films after. Hey, all you schmucks out there that didn't cast me in your films – you're going to regret it now!*

The man answers that of course they initially thought about Papa.

'But there will be loads of older men delivering speeches that night, so it would be good to see a woman up there. And we noticed that you'd be attending the banquet anyway, and that you are an actress. What is your relationship to Dylan?'

This eternal question.

'Well . . . I don't know him personally, but since everyone around Papa is interested in him, he's always been present in my life. By the way, will the speech be in Swedish or in English?'

Again, his soft voice through the receiver:

'Yes, of course it will be in English.'

Oh, why didn't Papa force me to speak English with him when I was little? Why in the seventies was it considered harmful for children to learn more than one language? My answer comes a millisecond too late:

'I understand.'

There it goes. I can see it slipping through my fingers. But the man on the other end continues asking questions. He wants to know in detail how I, however little, am acquainted with Dylan. I tell him again how Dylan has always been a presence in my life, but that it's sad sometimes that the Dylan thing overshadows all the other stuff Papa has done. I talk too much. The only thing he really wants to know is if I have a 'private' relationship to Bob Dylan, if I 'really' know him. I continue dancing around the question until finally he asks:

'So, would you be interested in making the speech?'

'I speak better English than most Swedes . . .'

'Yes, we certainly do need someone who speaks impeccable English.'

Carefully he brings up the question of Papa.

'How is your father? Do you think he could manage a situation like this? The banquet does go on for many hours.'

'It should absolutely be Papa who reads the speech. But yeah, he's eighty-eight years old and perhaps a little confused . . .'

The man knows how to choose his words. If this was a fairy tale he would have been cast as the fox.

'What's there to worry about?'

'Well . . . He might read the same line twice, or if it's several pages, he might miss a page . . . But listen! Wouldn't it be nice if Papa and I read the speech together?'

He has all the information he needs. Now he wants to talk things over with his colleagues and closes by telling me that this is hot stuff for the media.

'You can absolutely not tell anyone about this conversation.'

I promise. We hang up. All is silent. Grocery bags and weekday chores lean up against my legs.

The next day I can't take it anymore. I call one of my friends. She gasps:

'How could you do something so stupid? This is all because you're a woman!'

She shouts:

'Do you know what horrible English our Swedish politicians speak!'

If anyone knows, it would be her. She tells me that I need to email them right away.

'Write and tell them that you'd be honoured to do it and that you can get an American dialogue coach to help with your pronunciation. We can pretend my husband is one!'

I listen, copy all her professional-sounding phrases into an email, exactly the way she told me, and press send.

The answer comes a couple of days later. I'm home alone, my laptop on the kitchen table with the smears and crumbs from breakfast.

> Hello,
>
> We'd like to thank you for your enthusiasm and good-will, but we've decided upon another way to approach the question of the speech. We appreciate your thoughtful suggestions and hope that now you will enjoy the banquet as a guest instead.

I go into the bedroom. Lie down on the bed. Let a few tears wet my pillow. And then it passes.

1983

The Royal Dramatic Theatre is looking for a nine-year-old girl for a production of *A Dream Play*. It's by August Strindberg. Papa saw the advertisement in the newspaper, pasted it in my diary and sent them a letter and a photo. Now they've called me for an audition, and I'm dressed in my nicest dress. It's the one with all the ruffles I got from my rich cousins in America. They have a Coca-Cola machine in their kitchen. We walk up to the stage entrance, are met by a woman with a thick, loose-leaf binder and a whole bunch of keys. We go up in the lift.

'Why don't you just wait here,' she says when we have arrived. 'The director will come and get you in a few minutes.'

I smile as sweetly as I can.

We sit. A couple of minutes later a door opens and a red-cheeked girl looking a lot like me skips through. She hops over to her mother who waits a few metres away. Now the director opens his notebook and reads my name out loud. He can't pronounce it. Nobody can. I stand up immediately and walk straight into the room. Bright light. Loads of windows. Two grown-ups sit behind a very long desk. There's a camera there too. The director hunches down next to me:

'As you know, we're testing you for a role in a play here at the Royal Dramatic Theatre. Could you stand there, in the middle of the floor?'

I do everything he says, listening carefully.

'We are wondering . . . what would you do if there was a horrible witch chasing you? That's what we want you to show us when I say "action". That's when you start to improvise. Do you know what improvise means?'

I know what it means; I learned it in theatre lessons.

He sits with the others behind the big desk, stares right at my eyes, calls out very clearly:

'Aaaand action!'

I look right, then left; that's what you do when you're afraid. After that I run as fast as I can and throw myself under a table at the back of the stage. I curl myself into an invisible ball, hiding my face between my knees, closing my eyes as hard as I can. The room is silent. I soon understand that I made a really bad decision. It's boring to watch a girl sitting under a table with her eyes closed. But I can't think of anything better. I just sit there, panting like I was afraid until the man says:

'Thanks! You can come out now.'

I'm led out of the room.

Papa and I take the lift down. He asks:

'How did it go?'

'Really bad.'

As we walk back to the park I can't hold back the tears. I'm ashamed that I was so bad in there. I know that I'll never get that role. Even if I haven't given up hoping. Papa puts a hand on my shoulder and says, 'Well, well', that we should go and buy ice cream and eat them on a bench in the sun.

2010

Papa needs to get a pension. Now. If he doesn't, he'll lose the store. He owes the printer, the dentist and a good friend, several thousand kronor. He is eighty-two and should have started collecting his pension almost twenty years ago. But all he ever did was laugh and say, 'Pension? What's that?'

There's no one else who can fix this except for me, no one else who can contact the authorities, make the difficult phone calls, fill out complicated applications. I'm the one that will have to confess, to be accountable for all the tax he never paid, all the income declarations he never sent. He has almost never touched an official Swedish paper. Somehow, he's managed to dodge the Swedish state for over thirty years. Still, he's been living in Sweden the whole time, has a daughter that went to school and daycare here, got the Golden Boot from *Dagens Nyheter*, has been interviewed on television, on radio, learned Swedish, has been featured in Swedish magazines and published one of his own.

How can I ever explain, make the state bureaucrats understand? What can I do to stop my hands and knees from shaking every time I need to pick up the phone? But the store costs ten thousand kronor a month in rent and it would be impossible for me to carry that kind of expense. It's a wonder he's been able to survive this long. I need to do something about this situation. As quickly as possible.

I find a therapist. My plan is to let her hold my hand throughout the whole process. On the very first visit I blow my nose through every tissue in the white box on the table between us. I cry too much. Cry so I'm almost sick. She thinks I must be exhausted, on the verge of a total break-down. But I'm crying because she frightens me. She doesn't look how I expected her to. I'm crying because in the toilet there were vanilla-scented candles, because classical music was playing in the waiting room, and you could choose a latte or a macchiato from the stainless-steel coffee machine. I'm convulsing and snivelling because the floors are parquet and her bookshelves have glass doors. It's all much too nice. Not at all like me. I'm crying because she'll cost me a thou-sand kronor for every forty-five minutes and what I really need is years of hours.

We don't become close, she and I, but she does hold my hand. With her support I manage to fill in the endless number of forms and make thousands of phone calls to the tax authorities without feeling too much shame. The best advice she gives me is childish but effective. I should pretend that I'm a detective; every 'no' should be interpreted as a clue leading me closer to that pension. She helps me realize that it's better to receive a negative response because then I become aware of what my case is missing. A 'no' forces me to sharpen my wit. She helps me transform no into yes, to be more suspicious of a yes than a no.

Six months later Papa and I are sitting on the Swedish Tax Agency's hard chairs. Papa is about to be registered. We have an appointment, but I take a ticket for the queue, just to be sure. I hold his passport, his residence permit, some freshly taken snapshots, my own identity card and birth certificate, in a plastic document sleeve. Papa has brought a paper bag; it's full of cuttings from newspapers, diaries and old issues of his own magazine. In that bag he has thirty years of evidence. This is one of those days that counts. I sweat. Up until now I've got far on what's almost true, the fact that Papa has some kind of phobia of authorities. He, on his side, claims that he has contributed to Swedish culture without ever having received any financial support, neither as a business nor as a private person.

At last it's our turn to present ourselves at counter number nine. I push Papa's passport through the slot in the glass window that separates us from the civil servant, unsure whether I should speak, or let Papa begin. He stands silent, playing dumb. By now, I've learned the necessary lingo and can look the lady right in the eye. She glances up at Papa, ascertaining that he is the same person as pictured on the passport, then she turns to me. It only took one glance for her to determine that it was me and not Papa she should talk to.

Papa clears his throat and presses closer to the partition.

Now he wants to join in, wants to charm and show everything that's in his bag. He tries to pass through the slot at the bottom of the window article after article, with headlines like 'Dagens Nyheter congratulates Izzy Young', and issues of his newsletter spanning several years. One document after another. The lady doesn't have the time for this and is hesitant to even touch Papa's stuff.

'Just a second. I'll find a colleague better equipped to handle your case,' she says and snaps the slot closed.

As soon as she's out of sight I stuff all of Papa's documents back into his paper bag and hiss:

'You have to let *me* handle this!'

Papa is silent and I just manage to hide the paper bag so that it's not visible from behind the counter when an energetic official in a suit settles into the chair behind the window. Humming, he picks up Papa's passport and opens it. When he reads the name, his eyes grow wide:

'You're Izzy Young! Don't you know Bob Dylan?'

Ten minutes later we go out through the heavy Tax Agency gates and Papa laughs:

'You see? I know how to talk!'

He puts an arm around my shoulder and asks if I have time to stop for a coffee.

'Thank you, Papa, but I need to go home now. I need to rest.'

Finally, the letter arrives. Papa's application has been approved. He won't be getting his pension retroactively and it won't be enough for both the apartment and the store, but it's a big step in the right direction. Papa's friend Buffalo steps in, and from now on he and I handle all Papa's bureaucracy together. For a couple of years we manage, in some miraculous way, to scrape together enough to cover both rents. A benefit concert is arranged and Papa, reluctantly, sells two handwritten song texts that Dylan gave him. Sometime later he's also forced to sell off a portion of his beloved collection of poetry books from the fifties and sixties. Those tattered volumes that stood on the shelves below the pipes in the basement, first editions, some with dedications written by Jack Kerouac, Allen Ginsberg and other friends. Thank heavens those pipes never leaked. But even the funds from these sales begin to run dry and soon Buffalo says:

'There's only enough money now to pay the rent for another five months. We might have to let go of the lease.'

Papa says:

'I'll just have to work harder. I'll put on more concerts.'

Both Buffalo and I know that it could never be enough. What Papa pulls in on concerts can never pay the rent.

We get in touch with the Royal Library and the Swedish Music Archives; would they consider purchasing Papa's folk-music library? They visit the store, cast a dubious eye on the shelves full of books, pull out some that are of particular interest and say that they might be able to house his collection, but only if they can acquire it for free. Their shelves are all full as it is. When they leave Papa calls them worthless bureaucrats.

'I've invested every penny I ever made in these books. Fucking idiots.'

He laughs, but I know deep down it hurts him.

Instead, an American folk-music professor turns out to be the store's saviour. He is a friend of Papa's and is anxious for this rich collection to remain intact. Thanks to him the Library of Congress, the place where Papa always dreamed his archives might end up, get in touch. They want to buy part of Papa's archive and are willing to pay good money. When I call to share the news, Papa responds in a thin, light voice:

'This proves that I'm important, that I was doing the right thing all along.'

He gasps for breath.

'I'll be famous.'

Some weeks later an American dealer in antique books walks into the store. He is representing the Library of Congress. He has jetlag but manages, surprisingly, to calm Papa, who is muttering distrustfully and can no longer keep up with what's going on around him.

The very next day the man begins his work. Diaries, newspapers, letters, flyers, fanzines, newspaper clippings, posters and concert programmes that used to lay jumbled up in drawers or disintegrating folders are now meticulously organized, one by one, in boxes. From time to time the dealer lifts a paper up to the light and exclaims:

'This is invaluable. You'd never find anything like this anywhere else.'

The journals are especially unique; small notebooks in which Papa has written about everyone who's passed through the store, what they said, what they were reading and what songs they were playing. And probably everything they ever bought. Papa sits at the marble table and watches over the proceedings. When the dealer mounts the ladder to reach the binders on the top shelf, Papa points to his back saying:

'Who is this guy taking all my stuff? Am I getting paid?'

Papa demands to see and discuss every document before it goes into the boxes. He doesn't realize that the American has three days in which to inventory thousands of books and numerous drawers stuffed with papers. Buffalo and I alternate days playing diplomat and running out to buy coffee. With a hot cup of coffee and a bun under his nose Papa has an easier time relaxing; he can even toss a joke in the direction of the American.

Day two, fortified by cake, they unexpectedly start to sing a popular American tune together. By the morning of the third day, thirty-six boxes have been filled with over three hundred kilos of books and papers. Still, looking up at the shelves, you can barely see a difference. The dealer packs the last items deemed important, the shipment is scheduled for pick-up in a couple of hours.

Papa wants this and at the same time he doesn't. When the truck arrives and the carefully sealed boxes are piled on the pavement outside, he steps out in shirtsleeves. He caresses the boxes gently and kisses them goodbye before they get piled on a pallet and are fork-lifted into the truck. He sighs and whispers, 'Bye, bye.' I take his hand in mine, that big, strong hand that's always so warm:

'This is exactly what you've been dreaming about. Now your collection is on its way to the biggest and most beautiful library in the United States. It will be there for ever for people to see.'

'Well, well' is all he says, taking a deep breath and turning back into the store.

The American says his farewells and gets a real kiss on the cheek from Papa. Buffalo, Papa and I stay behind, drinking coffee. We eat cakes, look up at the bookcases. Only a few gaps are clearly visible, the spaces where several books have been taken from the same place. There is still an incredible amount of books left. Papa stands and walks across the room to the shelves, carefully measures one of the gaps with spread fingers. He turns and faces us with a wide smile:

'Now I know what I'm going to do! I'll go to the used-book market on Drottninggatan on Sunday, buy some new books and make my library even better.'

1983

Papa and I spend the whole day at the library. We usually hang out here at weekends or when I don't have school. I stand in my socks, with my shoes off, shuffling through empty album covers stored in large boxes. I choose the ones I like most and take the album covers to the loan desk. The librarian is standing there. It's her job to lend out books and to put records on the record players. All the records are in sleeves with numbers on the shelf behind her. I listen to them, one after the other. Sitting, shoes off, feet pulled up on the green sofa, huge earphones, twisting the cable between my fingers.

She plays records for me all day long, turning them over when one side is finished. Sometimes Papa goes off somewhere, leaving me alone for an hour, maybe two. I like it. The librarian and I don't say much to each other, but she always flashes me a secret smile whenever we come in. I think she likes me.

Now she walks around the room banging on a small cymbal. That means they'll soon be closing. She doesn't really need to do it; Papa and I are the only ones left. Papa whispers:

'You have to say thank you to her. Say thank you.'

I don't want to. I drag my feet, run my fingers across the shelves and the spines of the books. Papa tries pushing me towards the loan desk, it's so very important that I say 'thank you'. He'll get angry soon, I feel it in the air. I run past the librarian, out into the cloakroom where my jacket is hanging. I pick up speed, in my socks I can glide several metres. Papa is silent. I tie my shoes. The librarian stands by the outer door now, waiting to lock it once we're outside. Papa nudges me in the side, looks at me sternly; I have another chance now. But my lips won't move. I can't. I slip innocently past her dangling keychain and into the square outside. I don't even say goodbye.

Outside, pigeons are flying across a clear blue sky and the library steps are a thousand high. I walk on ahead, Papa a few steps behind me. I'm singing, humming. Then all at once he slaps me. On the shoulder. Not hard really, but still I gasp for breath. It's never, ever happened before. That he's hit me. I keep walking, staring ahead, pretending like nothing happened. I hope nobody saw it. Hitting a child is against the law. But deep inside I know he's right. I should have said thank you to her, the nice librarian who'd been helping me all day long. I should have done it, even if I didn't want to.

2016

Snow has fallen during the night turning grey November to blinding white. Papa spent the night at our place and the kids are now at school and pre-school. We have some time for ourselves. Unable to relax, I stand at the sink busying myself with the breakfast dishes. He sits at the kitchen table bending over the thin journal he always carries in his pocket. We're listening to blues, Karen Dalton. Her voice so intense, so drenched in sorrow. You can't escape from it. It's like gravel and like velvet. The first time I heard her voice I couldn't believe that she was both white and young. I still can't really understand it.

Some people are coming today to interview Papa about Dalton and he's nervous, says he didn't know her so well and that he doesn't have a lot to say. I think he's right; as far as I know she was an introvert and probably didn't hang out in the New York store a lot. I keep playing song after song, hoping he might remember a bit more for the interview. We eat fresh, ripe mango cut in pieces. Karen Dalton is singing for us. The trees outside are all white.

Goodbye, oh my old sweethearts and pals.
I'm goin' away
I may come back to see you, darling
Some old rainy rainy day

By evening, the snowfall has brought Stockholm to a standstill. Cars aren't going anywhere and the metro stopped working hours ago. When I call Papa to see how the interview went he asks me if he can sleep overnight in the store. I tell him I understand, imagining how difficult it would be for him to get home.

'Okay, do it.'

He thanks me.

Should I venture out, sliding across the snowdrifts to pick him up? But he seemed totally happy to have been allowed to sleep in the store. Almost elated. I think that he probably doesn't have anything there for breakfast. Does he even have a blanket? If anyone sees him sleeping in the store I'll feel ashamed. Not for his sake, but for my own. Because I didn't go and pick him up. Because I left my father. My papa-child. But tonight I don't have the energy and I'm longing for my own, real children. I want to give them my time, give myself time. When he's around it's sometimes difficult. I'm being pulled in three different directions, four if I count Lasse. Or ten if I count my friends.

Papa wrote a poem once about me working as an actress. He wrote it in the form of a letter in which he observes me on stage and how present I was in the character I was playing. The final line in the poem is directed straight to me: 'And don't forget to live your own life too.' I think he probably could have said that to me right now as well. Don't forget to live your own life. Still, it remains the one thing that is most forbidden.

He doesn't answer the phone the next morning. Immediately I start thinking of all the places he might be. Still asleep in that dark cellar, on the toilet perhaps, maybe drinking coffee in one of the nearby cafés or dead in a snowbank. Maybe he changed his mind and went to his apartment anyway. Though I doubt it.

I know that cellar where he is probably sleeping right now. It's warm there. I can hear the water flowing through the pipes that hang under the ceiling. How it sometimes gurgles. I know what it sounds like in there when the neighbours visit their basement storerooms, how dirty the fridge is and how millions of silverfish scurry like lightning for cover the second you turn on the fluorescent ceiling lights. I know that I mostly slept soundly there when I was small. Unless someone started to pull at the upstairs door in the middle of the night.

1984

Papa picked me up after school and now we're in the staircase of our building. We can't open the door to our apartment. Papa's key doesn't fit into the keyhole anymore. It's been coming for a while now; the building is slated for renovation, apartments to be turned into offices. We don't own the contract ourselves; it belongs to the people on the other side of the wall who we kind of live in a commune with. They were allowed to move to another apartment, but it couldn't be arranged for me and Papa. We stayed in the apartment even though construction workers began to tear down the walls where our neighbours used to live. Me and my commune sister hated these builders. Before she moved away we built a horse out of cardboard and tied it next to their things. We smeared evil-smelling stuff on their tools, like garlic oil, and wrote that they were stupid. We even wrote on the wall of her bedroom where she was never allowed to draw: WE WANT TO STAY HERE!

But now our key doesn't fit anymore.

Papa and I walk down the steps made of stone, that I have loved and been running up and down since I was little. We walk out on to Kocksgatan, and we never go back again. We go to the store. Walk down another flight of stairs, stairs that I also know, also like. Stairs that lead down to the cellar. It's fairly large but there aren't any windows. The floor and the walls are stone. The floor is painted grey and the walls are kind of white. There are paintings as well, and posters. And loads of books. On one of the paintings the word 'YAZZ' is scrawled and a group of stick figures play trumpets. Papa had already moved some of our stuff in; two beds, my teddy and a doll. I'm too big for those things now really; I'm ten. Still, I'm happy that they're here.

We move from a sunny two-bedroom apartment on the third floor with a gas cooker and a thousand curious corners and cupboards to a forbidden cellar with a micro-wave oven. I duck when I walk past it because I'm scared of radiation.

For the next three years we live in different places, or in the cellar. Hidden and illicit but otherwise safe and quite hap-pily housed. Living in other people's apartments is worse, among all their things and their smells. They probably think that they're being nice to us by loaning us their apartments, helping me and Papa. But I don't like their homes. Not the nice ones or the ugly ones. Nor the ones with lots of furniture or those that are empty. Nothing in those places belongs to me. I don't want to look at their photos, their paintings, their clocks. I want my own medicine cabinet, not to share one with someone who's away on holiday and who I hardly know. My toothbrush next to their old ones.

2016

We take the lift down to the platform at Mariatorget's metro station. Papa brags about being smart by not taking the steps:

'You see? I am careful!'

I tell him that it's very good and see my reflection in the lift's window. My face looks different when I'm wearing glasses. I've just got over an eye infection and don't want to put in contact lenses. We're not comfortable, not used to standing next to each other in metro lifts.

'So, what are you working with?' he asks, to break the silence.

I look up, surprised, mumble that I mostly record audiobooks, that sometimes I have acting jobs and that I write.

'Aha . . .' He stares through the lift window.

My body feels itchy. I want the lift to stop.

Once out on the platform I catch his eye.

'Papa, you know that I'm your daughter, right?'

He jumps slightly.

'Oh sorry, I didn't recognize you with those glasses.'

I look him firmly in the eye.

'You can forget everything, just don't forget me.'

'I promise.'

I take his hand in mine, feel both warm and angry as we step on to the train. We sit facing one another and I stuff my glasses into my backpack with all the books and other stuff. I look at him. Without my glasses he's a little fuzzy. He smiles. He recognizes me.

2016

The average cost of hiring a tuxedo is about 1,500 kronor, excluding the dress shoes. At Albertina's Tailor and Dry Cleaners, you can get a complete black-tie package for 990 kronor. I don't dare choose the cheaper alternative. I have a preconception that it won't fit Papa properly or that the style would be out of fashion. I have no idea how a tuxedo is supposed to fit. It's probably better to go for an expensive one. I choose Östermalm's Dress and Tuxedo on the exclusive side of town. It'll be worth the 2200 kronor. This is once in a lifetime.

We take the metro across town. Papa spent the night at my place so I know he's clean and is wearing fresh underwear. He doesn't really understand what we're doing or why, but he's happy to be spending time with me. After we have tried on the tuxedo we'll go for coffee and cakes. That he understands without a problem.

In the shop he starts fiddling with the shirts. He pulls the price tags up to his eye, squints and looks at me in shock:

'Who buys this kind of shit?'

The floor is made of wood, and exclusive items of clothing sit by themselves, carefully folded, on every shelf. Soft music streams from the speakers. There is an occasional hiss from a steam iron in a small alcove where alterations are made. A mix of students and professors inhabit the shop, all of them going to the Nobel Banquet or the afterparty. We're invited to sit in the leather chairs in the back room. There's a serving trolley with bottles of whisky but I can't decide whether it's just for decoration.

When our turn comes Papa has a hard time getting up from the chair. He's getting physically weaker, making it harder for me to help him. A woman leads him to a cubicle with velvet curtains. He should undress so that she can take his measurements. He looks so naked, waiting in his underpants in that tiny cubicle.

After he's been measured the woman comes back with the clothing. She buttons the cufflinks and snaps the cummerbund. I watch carefully, committing each step of the dressing process to memory. Papa wonders where his own clothes are. For the fifth time I tell him:

'We're trying on the clothes that you're going to wear at the Nobel Prize Banquet. You know, the big party we're going to in a few weeks. We're only borrowing these.'

I point to the hook at the back of the cubicle:

'Your clothes are hanging right there.'

He immediately feels it when something doesn't fit just right and changes trousers several times before he's satisfied. Finally, he steps out into the store in full formal attire. He smiles in pretend surprise when he sees his reflection in the mirror and bursts out:

'Is that me? Nobody will recognize me!'

He starts tap-dancing and looks like Fred Astaire, just a little wobblier. Everyone in the store laughs. Now that we've found the right sizes he can have his coffee and something tasty on the side.

1984

I'm in the fourth grade and we haven't been living in the store's cellar for the last few months now. We've borrowed an apartment in Gröndal, a suburb. There is only one room and a tiny kitchen. The man who lives there is from Vietnam and he is in prison. For rape. The apartment is crowded with furniture. I sleep in a bed that creaks and Papa lies on a mattress crammed into a corner. In the bathroom, when you sit on the toilet, there's hardly enough room for your legs.

I think about it almost all the time. The man who usually lives here raped someone. Maybe even in the bed I'm sleeping in. I think it was his girlfriend. I've met him. It seems strange that such a small guy could rape. He had a big smile the few times that I met him in the store.

Gröndal is boring. Desperately boring. To get here you have to take a bus and there's almost no one ever on the streets. There's only one convenience store. Papa and I don't have anything to do one rainy day so we go in there. They sell tinned foods, crisps and the evening newspapers. The advertising board for one of the papers says that they've invented something fantastic. That if you rub a picture in the newspaper you'll be able to hear a song from Carola's new album. I pull on Papa's sleeve.

'We have to buy it, Papa, we just have to!'

I run all the way back to the apartment, jumping puddles with the newspaper safely tucked away under my jacket. I have to wait at the door because we only have one key.

Sitting at the kitchen table I start rubbing my finger over the photo of Carola. I do it carefully, just the way the arrows are showing, but no matter how much I rub I don't hear a sound. Papa gets impatient, grabs the paper and tells me that I have to move my finger the right way. He rubs and rubs until I'm afraid the newspaper is going to tear. Then we see it. Both of us. The date. 1 April. Equally foolish, we laugh all day long.

That evening Papa pours one and a half cups of cream into the blender, adds a banana, chocolate powder and some sugar and mixes it until it turns brown and fluffy. We eat it in silence. I have my chair pulled tight against the table so as not to bang the wall with the backrest. The mousse is smooth, but you can feel the undissolved sugar on your tongue. We wipe our fingers around the edges of our bowls, licking every last trace. Papa even wipes the blender clean with a thumb. In unison we shout: 'We don't eat like pigs; we are pigs!'

When we've turned out the light and gone to bed, I feel sick. Still, there's nothing tastier than Papa's special mousse.

2016

Nobel morning. Breakfast: cereal for the kids, I eat a sandwich standing up while writing today's schedule: Pick up Papa's medicines, drive over to his apartment in Fredhäll, meet the film crew there at eleven, make lunch.

On the way to the car I phone Papa:

'Hi, Papa, it's the Nobel Prize today!'

'Oh, wow, great!'

'I'm coming to get you in an hour.'

'I can't wait to see you.'

Stockholm is covered in snow. I drive carefully. It's Saturday morning and there are hardly any cars on the street yet. It's a lovely day for a Nobel party.

When I get out of the lift on Papa's floor the door to his apartment is wide open. I rush inside calling:

'Hello?'

All the lights are on. At first it's oddly silent, then a shuffling sound from the bedroom. A couple of 'hupp, hupps'. Then he's there, standing in the hallway. He's been waiting, letting the front door stand open, has no idea where we're going, but he smiles widely when he sees me. I take my shoes off. Today the place is clean, nothing sticky on the floor. Papa is freshly shaved and showered.

He wants to finish something that he was writing in his journal and sits down at the desk by the bedroom window. I plonk down on the bed. Wait. Snowflakes are falling outside and Papa is a silhouette against all the whiteness. He mumbles:

'Yesterday . . . like I always do, I read . . .'

A jumble of unconnected words, but he's focused. A room becomes so calm when someone's writing in it.

My green Golf carries us over the Västerbron back to the centre of town. I drive, Papa is in the passenger seat and two people from a Swedish film crew sit in the back. Another in a long stream of hopefuls that say they want to make a documentary film about Papa. The camera is tight against our necks as Papa delivers his usual speech about how healthy he is and all the rest of it. He asks several times what we're going to do. The fan hums, pumping heat. I repeat the day's schedule:

'First, we're going to my place and we'll eat lunch, then you're going to rest for a while, after that we'll get dressed, you'll wear that tuxedo . . .'

'What tuxedo? Is it mine?'

'No, we hired it the other day at that store behind the theatre. You can have it until Monday.'

He seems to think about this as we drive into Södermalm. I continue:

'After we dress, we'll take a taxi to the Concert Hall and attend the prize ceremony. When the prize ceremony is over we'll get a chartered bus to the Nobel Banquet at the City Hall. We'll have dinner there. It's going to be fantastic. The evening won't end until around midnight.'

Papa hums; he's more interested in pointing at houses and posters.

Home again. Lasse's taken the children off to the cinema so that we can have the apartment to ourselves. I help the film crew get settled, make lunch for me and Papa. They wait in the living room while we eat. Maybe I should have made lunch for them too? When we're finished eating I tell them they're welcome to have some fruit.

I make Papa lie down on mine and Lasse's bed, on the covers. I would like for him to sleep a while before the evening. He pats the blanket, sighs contentedly, puts the pillow under his head the way he likes it. I pull the thick velvet curtains, turning the winter light on Papa's face into sudden darkness. He lies on his back with his hands folded over his chest, eyes closed. I swallow, move on quickly, carefully close the sliding doors.

The film crew and I whisper in the living room as the doorbell chimes. Gio, the hair and make-up artist, arrives with a suitcase full of everything she needs. She fills the bathroom with brushes and make-up, saying that what I wish – to be a thousand times more beautiful but still look completely natural – is the hardest thing there is to do. She brushes and blow-dries, hides the dark circles, curls lashes, paints an almost imperceptible shade of cherry on my lips. The bathroom floor feels warm underneath our feet. Three-quarters of an hour later I look at myself in the bathroom mirror. There she is again, the beauty, even if she's still wearing sweatpants and a T-shirt.

At three o'clock I go to wake Papa. Careful not to mess up my hair, I open the curtains and stroke his cheek lightly. The winter light has already gone to bed. Three flights down, car headlights sweep the street, the ancient Luma light-bulb sign beams neon retro-yellow, competing in height with the ski slope on Hammarbybacken. Soon the moon will rise.

I turn on the bedside light, he puts his glasses on and once more I shut the door. The film crew will have to wait outside while Papa dresses. I protect. They respect.

When we last visited the clinic I found a nappy, a free sample, and smuggled it into my bag. It's just like a pair of briefs, padded on all sides and it pulls right up to the belly button. He agrees to wear it without any complaint. I take out the black, silk socks and ask him to sit down on the bed while I slip them on. His dry feet grab at the silk but nothing tears. Nobody will see them anyway and only an innocent beginner like me takes the bus all the way to Kungsholmen to find the right socks for 279 kronor. Because I think we have to have them. Because I don't want to feel ashamed if we've chosen the wrong accessories.

Soon Papa stands ready in his Nobel clothes: tailcoat, bow tie and, after a modicum of effort, cufflinks. He stands straight and tall, sees himself in the mirror, whispers:

'If only my mother could see me now . . .'

In the hallway Gio helps me pull on the gown. The film crew are ordered to look the other way. It's a challenge to get the dress on without damaging the material. First bra and knickers, then that whole extravagance around my head before metres of sequins and spangle-studded bobbinet cascade perfectly down my shoulders, breasts and stomach. I can't bend so Gio fastens the buckles on my heels. I pack a pair of paper-thin plastic gloves and a plastic apron in my handbag. Need to be prepared if Papa has an accident. With rubber bands and some twisting they make a tight roll. In my mind I send heartfelt thanks to my friend who organized this detail. Halfway out the door I decide to trust fate and leave the paper bag with Papa's spare dress trousers. It would be too ugly among all the beauty.

We step into the lift. The dress and the coat with the fake fur take up so much space that it's difficult to close the gate. Papa and I are squashed together with the mirrors reflecting back a hundred papas and a hundred daughters. The film crew take the stairs while we sail down. They meet us at the bottom with the camera. We step out, passing a neighbour with a laundry basket hurrying towards the laundry room:

'Hi! Oh, yeah, are you going to meet Bob Dylan?'

2003

Through the store window I see Papa holding court at his marble table. Yesterday, Dylan's annual tour blew through Stockholm and one of his entourage spent an hour in the store. Perhaps Papa and Dylan met this time.

Five gentlemen visitors sit circled around a mound of cakes and buns. The second I step into the room I understand why. Papa shouts:

'The concert was boring. Except for a few seconds when it sounded like a synagogue.'

A man who seems to be a journalist is taking notes:

'But you did get to meet him?'

'Of course! We talked for twenty minutes.'

Papa sighs, irritated, curls a hand around his coffee cup and says they met by the tour bus.

When Dylan saw Papa he called out: 'Izzy, so good to see you! I wrote a chapter about you in my book.' One of the men opens his eyes wide and leans in closer:

'What did you say then?'

Papa laughs, shoulders shaking, says he told Dylan 'he was

full of shit, he promised he would write that book back in 1962.' The men gape.

'And then I grabbed his cheeks and pinched them, like a Jewish mother does.' Papa, hands grabbing air, demonstrates the firm grip he had on Dylan's cheeks.

'He looked like a kid. He really did!'

The visitors chuckle, feel like they belong to the inner circle now, wait for the show to continue. But Papa sees me at the door:

'Enough with all the questions! Now I want to be with my daughter.'

I say hi to everyone, walk up to Papa. He kisses me with cardamom-covered lips and I wipe clean the crumbs he deposits on both my cheeks.

'I have something important to tell you,' he whispers before turning back to his audience. 'Sorry, guys, you'll have to go now!'

None of them show the slightest intention of moving on. They lean back, sip their coffees, grab another piece of Danish. Papa stands and points towards the door:

'Get out of here! You never buy anything anyway!'

Someone knocks over a cup and the others laugh. Their eyes pass embarrassed over the few objects for sale in the store windows: a pile of used CDs, a photocopied collection of poems, accordion music sheets and an old postcard showing a woman in traditional dress holding a nyckelharpa.

The journalist clears his throat.

'But there's got to be more to tell?'

'NO!'

Now Papa starts shouting that the journalist should be writing about *Swedish* folk music instead, that nobody in this country gives a damn about their cultural heritage, that if the Swedish government didn't force Swedish national radio to play a certain percentage of Swedish music, they wouldn't bother with it at all:

'It's crazy! Don't you idiots get it?!'

He points to his bookshelves, spraying saliva as he screams that no one ever looks at his books about Swedish folk music.

'All you fucking Swedes ever want is American shit! You won't pay a penny to see some Swedish culture, but you'll spend a thousand kronor on a rock concert, *no* problem!'

The convivial atmosphere has evaporated completely. Guests gather bags and briefcases. Someone grabs another muffin on his way to the door. Papa becomes contrite and throws his arms open.

'Come back some other day.'

And just before the door finally closes, he roars:

'But then you have to buy something!'

He waves at them through the windows, an exaggerated smile, muttering at the same time 'cocksuckers' while he shuffles off to fill his coffee cup.

Back again, he is careful about dividing the last of the cake. He tells me that he'd only had one earlier, reassuring the daughter who worries about his sugar consumption. Calmer now, after a few sips of coffee, he turns to me:

'You know what?'

'No, Papa, what?'

He looks me deep in the eyes, savouring the moment, and finally says, 'You know Dylan asked me where my estate was.' We laugh, spraying crumbs across the table. Papa catches his breath and looks at me again, his eyes glistening:

'And then when he understood that I'm practically living on the street he said he wants to send me something . . .'

The telephone on the desk rings and out of habit I get up and answer. I lift the receiver, which over the years has acquired a patina of grease from cake, butter, smoked salmon and coffee. It's Dylan's manager. Papa rushes over to take the call. I sit at the table, picking at the last crumbs of cake with the tip of my finger as Papa says:

'Good.'

'All right.'

And then laughing:

'So what? Everybody likes meeting me.'

When the call is over, I ask Papa what it was all about. He tells me that the manager called to say that Dylan was reeeeeally happy about meeting him. Papa looks out the window, drums his fingers on the coffee cup, stares up the street to see if the postman is coming. Always the high point of the day.

The weeks that follow are given up to speculation about what Dylan is going to send. Papa discusses this with friends who pass by, while each morning waiting eagerly for the post. Then comes the day. Papa opens a statement from his bank detailing a deposit of three thousand dollars from the United States. He stares at the paper, lifts his glasses and holds it close to his eyes, trying to see if he might have read it wrong.

'Peanuts,' he says. 'I would have been much happier if he wrote me a letter or sent me a poem. That would have been real.'

1985

I pretend I need to go to the toilet. Raise my hand. Get an okay from the teacher. My pulse is racing and I swallow several times. Our jackets hang outside the classroom. Carefully, I close the door behind me. I'm all alone in the hallway. I hear the teacher's voice as the lesson continues. I make my way to the coats hanging on their hooks in the hallway. With swift fingers I excavate my schoolmates' pockets filled with fluff and gravel. It's hard to breathe. I find a strip of bus tickets, two unused coupons and a pair of ten-kronor notes. I have no pockets in my skirt so I scrunch everything in the palm of my hand. With shaking legs I hurry into the toilets, flush so it sounds like I was in there for real. Looking in the mirror I can see my heart beating right through my jumper.

Back in the classroom I slide into my chair, hiding what I've taken under my bum. At breaktime I'll smuggle it into my backpack. I'm looking down the whole time to make sure nothing sticks out. I pray to God that no one notices anything missing before they get home. I'll tell Papa about my amazing luck, how I found it all in the gutter. He'll believe me because just this week we found a whole packet of oatmeal cookies by the entrance to a building. Now we have cookies that will last for weeks.

2016

We set off for the Concert Hall as if in a whirl, wave at the film crew through the taxi's windows. My dress fills the back seat, glitters like the streetlights and the water surrounding Stockholm. Papa sits next to me under a cloud of bobbinet; he leans back in the seat and looks out at the falling snow. We glide silently through town until the car pulls into the market square at Hötorget. All the market stalls are gone for the day. A man in a reflective vest directs traffic over the cobblestones. I see through the window the blue facade of the Concert Hall, the illuminated fountain. The driver helps us out of the taxi. Papa has trouble finding his legs and I need a hand with my enormous gown. The wind stiffens and picks up snow. We struggle towards the hall's entrance. I gather my dress in my arms and feel the cold air whipping my bare legs.

Our names are checked against lists and we join the stream of gala-attired guests up the stairs. Standing in line at the cloakroom, like everyone else, we reveal what we've chosen to wear on this auspicious evening. All the men look the same, dressed in black and white, either tails or dinner jackets. There's more variation among us women. A hum of expectancy fills the foyer. Gigantic chandeliers hang from the ceiling over us.

Our seats are in the second balcony, close to the middle. On the way up the black marble staircase we stop and look at the crowd mingling below us. My dress is the most beautiful of them all. I lift the gown walking up the stairs. Papa holds my hand and with his other hand grabs the banister.

'There's something wrong with these shoes! I can't walk in them,' he says, stressed, shuffling forward.

People call out 'Izzy!' but no other words follow. I don't recognize anyone and neither does Papa. We find our seats and look down on the stage. The floor is covered in deep-blue carpeting and twenty thousand pink roses decorate the back wall. I wonder what it smells like up close. The stage design, I read this in the morning paper, takes inspiration from the cherry-blossom festival in Japan. Members of the Swedish Academy sit in armchairs, chatting. The permanent secretary is towering in front of them. I see something of myself in the way she occupies her space, pretending nothing is out of the ordinary. I'm still not sure if it was her on the phone two months ago, demanding Dylan's phone number. She looks confident in her dress with patterns of huge flowers, sweeping across the stage floor.

I glance at Papa in his Concert Hall seat. In his starched white shirt and white bow tie, he looks as if he's sat at hundreds of banquets before this. Not a hair out of place.

A drum roll. The royal family step in from one side of the stage. Papa takes my hand and whispers:

'Oh boy.'

We giggle, both of us. It's like going to the theatre except this is real. The conductor, dressed in a black ball gown, winds the orchestra with her baton. Mozart.

The tail-coated Nobel laureates take the stage, all except Dylan. They walk on and sit in low armchairs. At the end of the row, sitting closest to the audience, is a slight-built gentleman with chalk-white hair. He looks up at the side balconies and rubs his eyes. Grey-haired men give speech after speech. We hardly understand what they're talking about but, like the rest of the audience, we listen reverently. Hidden behind applause, Papa whispers:

'Look at all those prize winners. Not a single one is Black.'

'And not a woman among them,' I whisper back.

A fanfare is blown. The Nobel Prize in Physics is to be awarded to the thin man sitting on the end. He just stares at the ceiling and doesn't appear to understand where he is. The other laureates sit with their legs drawn up close to their chairs, but his legs are splayed out in front of him. The gentleman sitting next to him nudges him in the side and the thin scientist, confused, looks around the hall. Quickly a young student in a cap and white gloves is there helping the man to his feet. Another blast of trumpets fills the hall. It must have sounded like this in the 1800s. The King strides forward with the medal, while the young man, taking the ancient physicist by the arm, leads him regally towards the centre of the stage. The prize is handed over, the gentleman nods and gently taps the case holding the medal. When His Majesty motions for the laureate to take the box, he merely smiles, uncertain.

Everyone in the hall must understand what's happening. Does Papa? I'm afraid to turn and look. In haste, the student takes the medal while the old man's arms flop at his side. He looks so tiny as he's led away from the stage. The rest of us sit tight, among the flowers.

2011

Papa has an appointment for a memory evaluation. He doesn't entirely understand what this means, but he always does what I tell him. I was probably a bit vague when I explained it.

Mama, wishing to relieve me of some of the burden, takes him through all the tests. She tells me how he was rolled, lying on a trolley, into a brain scanner, and had to lie there for an hour. She sat in a chair next to the machine and read poetry for him while his brain was X- rayed from every angle. Coming out of the scanner he complained that it had made so much noise he had been afraid his head would explode.

In another test a woman asked Papa to remember three simple words and tell the time on a clock. He got angry and the room filled with a sour smell of sweat that doesn't normally belong to him. Like a stressed animal he tried to deliver the right answers. He's no longer able to live up to the clever schoolboy image he habitually emulates. They went out for coffee afterwards. Mama was also shaken.

I'm thankful that I didn't have to be part of it. But later, I'm appointed a therapist at the memory centre and given stacks of brochures. The therapist is the same age as I am, wears a grey cardigan with huge buttons. He looks like they do in all the films. I only go there once. He can't give me what I need. The only thing I want is more time to be with Papa.

2016

Mama phones me. She's curious about what I'm writing and I tell her that it's memories of me and Papa. From when I was a kid, when I was a teenager and from now as a grown-up. She wonders what kind of tone the book has and how I plan to work with the text. I'm afraid that the magic will disappear if I talk about it. But most of all, I'm nervous about how she'll take the book not being about her.

1985

Papa is together with Kim who was once married to one of Sweden's richest men. Her neighbour owns Hennes & Mauritz. She lives in an enormous house in the rich neighbourhood of Djursholm, with a long driveway and a garage for the car. She has an apartment in the Old Town too, and a country home with pictures of flowers on all the walls. The house she mainly lives in is two-storeyed. She has a son named Walle. He's five and I'm ten. I play with him in their library where small lamps light every bookshelf. Papa and I still live in the store.

When there is a party, me and the other kids sit in Kim's kitchen. In another room the adults feast on cured salmon while we eat hotdogs with ketchup. When no one is looking Papa smuggles a bit of salmon to me, wrapped in a napkin, so that I can taste it too.

'Sssshh,' he says, holding a finger in front of his mouth. 'I think smoked salmon tastes better than the cured one.'

Often, when we eat dinner at her house, we have to eat more when we get back to the store. She serves so little.

Two tiny potatoes and a piece of chicken each. A drop of sauce on the side. I suppose that's how rich people eat; expensive but not nearly enough. Even though she has tons of money, she works at the Salvation Army store. I think she does it for free. She bought a new blue linoleum floor for the store and a large Karl Johan sofa upholstered in black leather with studs in silver. When Papa's newsletter comes from the printer and he needs to stuff three thousand copies into individual envelopes, he usually gets so tired that he lies down on the sofa and takes a nap. It's big enough for him to stretch out his whole body. I usually help out to put stamps on the envelopes; every one of them has to have a stamp.

They fuck. In the middle of the night. Often. They even do it sometimes while I'm playing with Walle. They close the door to her bedroom and Papa says they're going to talk.

Now, they're lying in Kim's room and I'm standing outside in the dark. There are creaking noises from in there and they're breathing strangely. I call out:

'Papa . . .'

They stop immediately.

Papa seems to be more in love with her than she is with him. She hardly ever wants to sit in a café and she only ever wants to travel by car, never by metro. When she visits and we eat lunch in the store she always pulls the curtains. Usually, when friends come by, Papa carries some chairs and a table out on to the pavement and we drink coffee in the shade of the big tree. People always say it's like an Italian film, which makes me think about Marcello Mastroianni. I've seen him in films. Kim wants to visit rose gardens in London and Papa wants to dance or go to concerts. She came with us one time to a Cornelis Vreeswijk concert in the Old Town.

But he is in love. Head over heels. Some of his best poems he's written to her. He writes poems to me too. They're better.

Walle and I are swimming and playing in a lake. He talks like an old man, but I like him anyway and pretend he's my little brother. The surface of the lake is smooth and the sun has turned pink above us. Kim and Papa are sitting on a cliff a few metres away. I look at them, wave. Papa waves back, but it's clear that he'd rather talk to her. When I turn back to continue playing I can't see Walle. The water is still and there are small bubbles coming from the bottom. Without thinking I dive down into the dark and cold, frantically searching. I can't see anything, but I wave my arms in front of me. At last my hands find the body. It's cold and slippery and just wants to glide from my grip. I manage to get my arms in under his. My legs become strangely strong. Still, I'm shaking when I pull him to the surface. His lips are blue, his eyes are frightened, then the coughing comes. It's true, everybody knows I saved Walle's life.

A few years later Kim breaks up with Papa and he never really understands why. When I ask him, he has no answer, he just keeps writing poems. Once we see her at the baroque theatre by Drottningholm Palace. She pretends that she doesn't recognize us. We stand on one side of the theatre and she is on the other with her girlfriends.

2016

A member of the Swedish Academy stands on the Concert Hall stage, ribbons and medallions dangling from his chest. He licks his lips and steps up to the podium:

'Your majesties, your royal highnesses, honourable Nobel Prize laureates, ladies and gentlemen. What brings about the great shifts in the world of literature?'

And with a smile he reads his speech in which he draws comparisons between Dylan and the Oracle of Delphi, Shakespeare and Rimbaud. Heavy bags underline his eyes, still he reads with passion, takes well-considered pauses. It's pleasant to listen to:

'If folks in the literary world grumble it might be wise to remind them that the gods themselves never write; they dance, and they sing.'

Everyone solemnly applauds Dylan, their eyes on the place on the stage where Dylan isn't standing. There's just a large white N projected on to the middle of the stage. Silence. A lone guitar and Patti Smith's haunting voice unexpectedly fills the hall. She stands on the choir balcony under the great organ, confident, no make-up. Her voice, so direct and present, sends shivers down my spine. No one sings the way she does. Straight to the heart. Papa takes my hand.

> *Oh, what did you see, my blue-eyed son?*
> *Oh, what did you see, my darling young one?*
> *I saw a newborn baby with wild wolves all around it*
> *I saw a highway of diamonds with nobody on it*
> *I saw a black branch with blood that kept drippin'*
> *I saw . . .*

Suddenly she's out of breath, stutters half a word and breathes erratically into the microphone. She says, 'Sorry, I am sorry,' and glances quickly towards the conductor. She tries again, a couple more chopped syllables escape from her lips. Then she breaks. There is only silence from the auditorium.

'I apologize, sorry. I'm so nervous.'

Like a schoolgirl she turns towards the audience and laughs, embarrassed. An intense applause follows. It feels like everybody loves her in that moment. She restarts the song, but is soon searching for the lyrics once again, not so much that people notice, but I see the small looks of concern she flashes towards the conductor. She doesn't give up. Her hoarse voice finds its path and soon a pedal-steel guitar comes in behind her. In time to the music she marches and lifts one fist in the air. When the entire orchestra is brought in and the music intensifies, every hair on my arms stands like spears. We cheer. Everybody cheers. Even Princess Victoria's face lights up in a big smile as she lifts her hands to applaud. It looks genuine. Patti is smiling too. She sits. Letting her grey hair fall over her face. In the middle of all this jubilation I catch myself thinking that if Patti could forget the lyrics, perhaps even I would have been forgiven if I had read Dylan's acceptance speech and stumbled over a word or two.

The orchestra thunders. The royal family stand for the singing of the Swedish national anthem, 'Thou Ancient, Thou Free'. We also stand with the rest of the audience, but only know the words to the chorus, humming along the best we can. The ceremony is over, the lights are brought up and everyone takes a deep breath. Papa thinks it's time to go home.

'No, Papa. Not for a good few hours yet. It's time for *food*!'

This brings him back to life.

'We just have to go to the toilets first.'

He says he doesn't need to go. Some journalists are standing close so I lower my voice:

'We are going to the toilets, both of us. We won't be allowed to leave the table during the entire banquet. It's going to take several hours . . .'

On the way, behind the stage Papa and I say hello to stagehands. Papa shouts:

'It was fantastic. Thank you!'

I wonder how many minutes we have before the chartered buses leave for City Hall.

In the toilets with Papa and my enormous ball gown. I try to get the jacket, the braces, trousers and everything else off without dragging my dress through the dirt on the floor too much. The situation is under control, for now there is no need for gloves. I don't want to risk anything happening to his tux so I stay with him in the cubicle. I'd planned it that way from the start. I won't let him out of my sight for a single moment this entire evening. When he finishes I make sure he washes his hands. Then I need to take care of myself, but I don't want Papa to go outside. The bobbinet skirt is hard to manage and he turns to face the wall while I lift it high over my ears in order to sit. He looks like such a gentleman, standing in his fancy clothes, facing into the corner.

In the Concert Hall foyer again we hurry towards the cloakroom. Papa grabs a few extra programmes on the way for his collection. An exuberant older man who was once Dylan's English teacher stuffs an extra programme into his pocket too. We laugh conspiratorially and shake hands before he too hurries towards the exit. No other guests remain.

Papa and I are the last to leave when we step out into the dark December evening. In front of the market hall's lighted windows a lone bus waits with its 'Chartered' sign lit. People on the street are snapping pictures with their phones. As the bus hisses and kneels to open its doors we climb aboard like film stars. We have it to ourselves. Two press photographers stand outside taking pictures and we laugh, getting a taste of what it would feel like to be the main attraction on the red carpet.

2016

The documentary film-maker from England has rented the main screen at the Grand. He is about to show his film about Papa. There are over a hundred of us waiting in the auditorium. Papa is eating a banana. When we arrived, the red carpet in front of the entrance was rolled out and people wanted to take pictures of themselves standing next to him. The wind tossed his hair and he hugged everyone who came over to say hello.

The film-maker gets up on stage before the screening begins. He thanks a whole bunch of famous people that I'm not sure he really knows; Martin Scorsese and Sean Penn, among others. He says that Papa is like his grandfather. A while ago, speaking with me in confidence, he claimed that Johnny Depp had agreed to play Papa in the docudrama he is planning to make. I don't know, it doesn't seem particularly believable. But with Papa you never really know.

The film is strange. Papa's voice is heard with images of the planet Saturn suspended in space and Jupiter floating by in slow motion. Papa reclines low in his seat, legs stretched out in front of him, tears streaming. He's moved at hearing his own stories on the screen. A woman who knows Papa sits behind us; she is also crying the whole time. Perhaps she's thinking about the imminence of death, or maybe that's what everyone is doing. Everybody but Papa? I don't know what I'm supposed to feel. Mostly I'm thinking about what I'm going to say to the film-maker afterwards. That the pictures are beautiful, that he succeeded in recording some nice anecdotes, that Papa loved the film? My body tingles uncomfortably. Maybe because it feels like I'm looking at an epitaph. Written by someone else. The sequences seem way too long, Papa talking, talking, talking, his movements and speech so obviously directed.

After the film a man pushes his way towards the film-maker and us to say hello. He has some tulips that have seen better days in his hand, probably bought in the grocery store. He presents himself as 'one of Papa's best friends', claiming that they are almost like brothers. I've seen him in the store a couple of times, but he certainly doesn't belong to the inner circle and I've never known him to help out with anything. I start to have trouble breathing. Why does everyone want to be part of our family when they're not?

It's become more obvious now that I'm a grown-up that many see Papa as a father figure. Perhaps it's because the door to his store is always open, because he, unlike most other people, takes the time. Sometimes it feels like they believe they're just as much his children as I am.

Walking home I'm holding Papa under the arm. He is happy but tired, walks unsteadily. It's one of the first summer nights and people are sitting outside. He's stopped by one person and then another, on the street or in the metro. All the way home there are people calling out 'Izzy!' Despite not being that well known he probably gets stopped as often as any Swedish pop star. They don't ask for his autograph; they want to wave and ask:

'Izzy! How is it going with Dylan?'

They jump up, leaving their beers on pavement tables. They want a hug, want him to remember who they are. Papa embraces them, kisses cheeks, shakes hands and promises to send them things just like he always does.

When I've gone to bed I close my eyes, see images and hear sounds from the film. A planet hovering in slow motion, Papa's voice recalling a story he's told many times before. How one night in 1950 he took a girl he had a crush on to the observatory to look at the stars. How afterwards he was invited to tag along to his very first square dance and met Margot Mayo who became his teacher. Mayo was one of the key personalities in the New York folk-dance scene. She had a huge collection of folk-music recordings and introduced Papa to musicians like Lead Belly. After that first lesson Papa was hooked. If you take him at his word, he was the best square-dance dancer in New York City after only three weeks. His passion for folk music had awakened and having Margot Mayo as his mentor soon propelled him into opening his store.

I watch as he dreams of the past and hear him say again and again that he discovered folk music one night while looking at the stars with Elsie.

1987

I don't have my own room in the store's basement. Papa and I share. But there is a cupboard down there where you can talk on the phone. I call my best friend and we talk for hours. Sometimes I call the HotLine. I tell mountains of lies. I say that I have big breasts and that I've been together with lots of guys. One time a man asks me:

'But listen, is it really true you're sixteen?'

My cheeks turn red and I get tangled up in his questions, refusing to admit that I'm thirteen years old. Finally I just hang up, hear Papa talking upstairs with a customer.

We don't have a shower, so we go to the tailor's shop around the corner. They're the best in Sweden for sewing traditional folk costumes and Lisa and Ajgul work there. I go in and see them a lot.

We shower one at a time. Papa thinks it's silly that I want to lock the door and be in the bathroom by myself:

'You don't have anything to hide,' he says and laughs.

I hate it when he laughs at me.

Other days I like being at the tailor's shop. The windows

are full of green plants and it smells of warm wool and hot irons. It's quiet, full of needles and thread. They sew small precious hats, wide skirts, belts and waistcoats. Silver buckles and brooches lie in drawers. Each particular region has its own special jewellery. Steam hisses when they iron the thick cloth that will be embroidered by Lisa's experienced fingers.

I'm often there after school, during holidays, sometimes whole afternoons before I scamper around the corner and back to the store. I sit high up on their workbenches, watching. I never touch the cloth. Never make a mess. I listen to the radio with Ajgul and with Lisa.

I'm good at this. Good at blending in. Adults like me and I'm more at ease with them than with friends at school. When I go there I never need to knock. I just push the heavy door open and step right inside. Sometimes Ajgul pinches my cheek, complains and says:

'You should wear short-short skirts. Do it now while your legs are so good-looking!'

She's from Mongolia and is always giving me a hug or a pat on the cheek. Sometimes she cooks chicken for me and Papa.

Nisse is the boss and owns the tailor's shop, but mostly he's in the apartment behind the room with all the sewing machines. He has a blonde beard and is so tall he has to duck as he goes through doors so he doesn't bump his head. He's nice, but when he tells jokes I almost never understand. When you look in their folk-costume catalogue you mostly only see pictures of Nisse. Lisa is his wife and she lives in the big apartment in the back too. It's their shower that we borrow.

In the bathroom next to the toilet there's a stack of porn magazines. It's strange that they lay there in the open, even on days they know Papa and I are coming. After I lock the door I leaf through them quickly. Need to be careful, can't take more time, nobody should know I've looked in them. A little disgusted and for a short time excited, I press myself against the bathroom rug. But most of all I'm puzzled. Shocked. How can she, Lisa, so nice and friendly, want to be with him? A weirdo who likes looking at dirty magazines. Doesn't it make her sad?

I shower then, as fast as I can, looking at the door the whole time in case it suddenly opens. I dry myself with the towel we brought with us, the one that Papa and I share, the one that smells like a skunk and needs washing. I want to get out of here. I want to be with Ajgul and Lisa.

2004

'I'll buy you an ice cream,' I say as we walk towards Mariatorget. But actually, there is something else that I want. I get us each a cone and the cold mist from the fountain sprays our frozen bodies. The linden trees are still bare. There, on our favourite bench, with sparrows scurrying around our feet, in the park where we've been going my entire life, I finally take a deep breath and say the proud words:

'Papa. I'm pregnant. The baby is coming in December.'

A tear, and then another one wets his cheek.

'Wow . . .'

He kisses me, says that everything is exactly how it should be. He lifts his glasses to wipe his eyes. We continue licking our ice creams, saying nothing. In the fountain, the Serpent of Midgard splashes water and the muscled hero Thor raises his hammer towards the heavens. We catch the first rays of spring sunlight, eyes closed. A thin spray from the serpent's mouth, tiny cascades with almost invisible rainbows, fall over us softly. Papa's eyes are firmly fixed on the fountain as he says he also has something important to tell me. He says that a lot, but this time there's a different tone in his voice. I punch him lightly on the shoulder:

'So, now you're going to say that you're pregnant too, ha, ha.'

Five minutes later we walk stiffly out of the park. I've just been told that I have an older brother. As soon as the door to the store closes behind me I catch fire, I shout, I beat and scream. I want to hit him, scratch his cheeks, throw chairs, overturn bookshelves, smash those huge storefront windows, cut and tear skin with sharp glass shards. He sits there silently, pitiful, lets my angry words whip his bowed head. I don't even know if he can hear me because my voice is no longer mine. It's shrill and almost insane.

My brother is apparently named like me.

Thilo. Philo.

He lives in Germany. And he's coming to Stockholm soon.

The summer throbs with dust and we're waiting in the cool of the bus terminal. Bus after bus from Arlanda and Bromma airports pull into the station. He'll be here soon. My older brother. He that neither of us has ever met. Papa says that Thilo's German mother wrote a letter and told him that a son had been born, but that she didn't want Papa to be involved. The way he tells it, he got the word just as he and my mother were about to move to Sweden. He never said anything to Mama, scared that she would leave him.

That's Papa's version.

Thilo and I have exchanged letters and photographs. I've examined him closely, his nose, his height, his eyes and his hands. There can be no doubt, he is Papa's son. Is he the only one? Papa has often bragged about the two hundred women he'd been with behind the curtain in the New York store. He met Thilo's mother at the wedding of one of his ex-girlfriends. They were apparently twin sisters. Papa and Thilo's mother only spent one night together. I don't know how much of this is true, but it isn't inconceivable.

The bus with my big brother on arrives. We go out on to the platform to meet him. My heart is thumping. I'm embarrassed, hot and agitated. What does one do? Through the bus window I catch sight of Thilo's face; he looks exactly like the photographs he sent me. As soon as the door glides open he flies down the two steps, throws his arms open, his bag hanging from his shoulder. He rushes towards us, shouts with a German accent:

'Izzy, Philo!'

There we are, in each other's arms for the very first time. He is tall, big, broad-shouldered. His wife Julia steps down off the bus behind him.

Minutes later we're all four of us sitting on a metro train. Thilo mostly just smiles and looks out the window. Papa looks at me. The women will have to take the lead in charting this meeting between father and son, brother and sister.

Back at the store Julia and Thilo examine with interest the bookshelves and all the stuff hanging on the walls. Papa and I sit in the window. He whispers behind their backs that he isn't really sure whether or not it is his son. He says he doesn't feel anything. I feel like punching him, rise quickly to stand beside Thilo, steal a look at his hands. This is my brother. I know him, and at the same time I don't.

We go to Djurgården. Share a picnic on the green grass. The sky is blue and pollen flies in the air. It's fairy-tale-like beautiful and I'm close to tears the whole time. We play with a ball like we're kids. We do the best we can.

I cry in Lasse's arms that night because I want something that I can never have. I want to have been that little sister, had that big brother. Maybe he would have played with me, helped me with my homework. I don't want it to be awkward. I want to hug him without him being an attractive, grown-up man. I want back what's been stolen.

Papa invites some friends for dinner the last evening Thilo is in Stockholm. We're all pitching in to cook in Papa's apartment in Fredhäll. Thilo is in the kitchen making *spätzle*. He's wearing Papa's apron and the pans on the cooker are steaming. Papa is making chopped liver from a recipe he learned from Grandma. It's nice to see them doing something practical together; it makes everything simpler. I'm scrubbing the kitchen cupboards, the toilet and the floor. Everything is dirty, sticky. Thilo wrinkles his brow when he sees me on my hands and knees and wonders what I'm doing. I'm not sure that I want him to see this. Everything that I've been cleaning all my life. All he never had to do. Perhaps I'm trying to take some of the sting out of Papa's betrayal towards his son by showing Thilo that it wasn't always easy for me either. I blush, quickly finding my feet, and throw the dirty tea towel in the rubbish. Tomorrow he's leaving. Still, here he is, standing in front of me in Papa's apron.

The doorbell rings and guests come in. None of them have ever been here before; Papa never meets people at home. Since we moved from the apartment on Kocksgatan when I was small, he's only met friends in the store. The food is served from a table next to the bed since we can't fit everybody in the kitchen. Someone sits in the armchair, others on kitchen chairs and some on the bed. I sit next to Thilo. So close we're almost touching. Papa clinks his glass and stands. He isn't accustomed to making speeches but today he's made an effort, written a few lines on paper:

'I want to talk about true *love*,' he says, looking in my direction. 'I love you, Philomène. Nobody can ever be as close as you and I.'

With tearful eyes he goes on to describe this unique father–daughter relationship. He's shameless. Stupid. Imbecilic. Seven guests applaud politely when he's done. I don't dare to look at Thilo or Julia.

Later, in the purple twilight by Fredhäll's metro station, I kick a rubbish bin. I want to kick it hard enough to leave a dent, but I'm afraid someone will see me. I hate him and feel shame deep down in my stomach.

The following day pigeons fly under the glass ceiling of the bus terminal. Julia and Thilo's bags stand ready at our café table. It's only the three of us. I decided that Papa shouldn't come. He was probably relieved. I'm relieved. Perhaps Thilo and Julia breathe freely for the first time since they arrived in Stockholm. The bus is leaving in fifteen minutes. Dry cinnamon buns lie untouched on paper plates. I hide my face in my hands, cry so much that I can hardly speak. They pat my cheek, are somewhat ill at ease, tell me it's not my fault. I say I know, but what your brain tells you is one thing and what your heart feels is another.

Thilo doesn't say very much; I can't decipher what he's feeling. Julia wants to take a picture. We stand with our backs against one of the terminal walls, arms around one another. My shoulder lands in his armpit. Our bodies have never been this close for this long. We smile at the camera, probably looking quite alike, quickly releasing one another when she's finished taking pictures.

They get on the bus and we say we'll stay in touch.

They wave. I wave. They leave. After that we only communicate sporadically.

2016

Our feet are like ice when we arrive at City Hall and hang up our coats. The walls in the Blue Hall are made of brick and the ceiling above the inner courtyard must be thirty metres high. The columns are majestically lit in blue tones. Golden coins, candelabras and flower arrangements decorate the long tables. Such an incredible number of ball gowns.

We're handed table placement booklets with the Nobel insignia embossed in gold on the cover. Up until now the seating arrangements have been kept secret. I phoned and requested a place close to Papa, concerned about his age. It takes a while before the seating chart makes any sense but when I crack the code, I cheer and give Papa a big hug:

'They've given us seats at the Swedish Academy's table. I fixed it. We get to sit next to each other!'

Papa tap-dances with delight in his too-big shoes.

Swedish national television is broadcasting live and the TV host points to table decorations while speaking into cameras that sweep the room mounted on cranes. The murmur of a thousand conversations makes it impossible to hear what anyone is saying; it looks like everyone is miming. We crisscross the room, weaving past other guests. Papa stumbles and mutters:

'These fucking shoes are gonna kill me.

There's hardly any room between the tables and the chairs are set out exactly in meticulous rows. I hold him under the arm. We finally find our table. It's in the middle of the hall, branching off from the Table of Honour. A writer with messy, slicked-back hair welcomes us with open arms. He acts the gentleman, easing my chair out when I sit. His most famous book, later a feature film, is about a young writer who possesses nothing other than a couple of old typewriters. He becomes friends with two boxer brothers. I think it was filmed in a fancy apartment close to where Papa has his store. The woman sitting on Papa's right-hand side is a famous poet; she laughs with half-closed eyes when she sees us. Her frizzy hair hangs over one eye. I have several volumes of her poems at home and have seen one of her plays at the Royal Dramatic Theatre. She is one of my absolute favourites.

The gentleman writer pushes my chair to the table and I check to see that the tails of Papa's jacket have settled in place correctly behind his chair. I've made an effort to research how they're supposed to hang.

'I'm hungry,' says Papa, staring at the hundreds of gold-wrapped Nobel chocolate coins decorating the table. I'm not quick enough to stop him from peeling the gold wrapper from one of them. The poet helps Papa stuff a healthy handful into his jacket pocket and even smuggles some into her own handbag:

'I'm saving these for my grandchildren,' she says.

Melted chocolate decorates one of Papa's fingers already. How long until the coins start melting in his jacket pocket?

The poet's hair is grey now. It's a pity. I loved her wild, red hair. But her eyes are still as bold as ever and when she and Papa lean close I wonder if they could ever fall in love. I know that a few years ago on a late-evening train from Uppsala to Stockholm they sat across from one another. They talked the whole way home. Papa phoned me the next day, his voice filled with excitement. He wanted to write a long letter to her; like a teenager he thought that maybe something would happen.

A waiter fills our glasses with champagne; it bubbles. A student announces from the stage that we should raise our glasses in a first ceremonial toast to His Majesty the King. We stand and the room is silent. Everyone lifts their glasses as the King asks us to toast Alfred Nobel. The room murmurs. I wonder if Lasse would have refused. He is always pointing out that Nobel was a war profiteer, that he built his fortune selling weapons, that his hands were drenched in blood.

Hundreds of waiters all dressed in white float down the great wide stairs carrying the appetizers. They hold one hand on their back and the other high in the air. One thousand three hundred people are served at the same time, exactly. An edible work of art graces each of our gold-rimmed white

Nobel porcelain plates. It is so beautifully presented that my hands fall to my knees. We wait for the Table of Honour to take the first bite. Although the writer beside me doesn't care, swipes his hair back and smacks his lips:

'Time to tuck in,' he says and grabs his fork.

I wait discreetly for the others to begin, unsure what to do with the fragile crispbread lying decoratively on top of the food. The Swedish Academy members who are sitting all around us take the silverware that is farthest from the plate and expertly shift the bread to the side. I help Papa lay the cloth napkin across his knees.

When the waiter fills our water glasses I ask what the topping on each of the tiny round baskets are. He bends and whispers close to my ear:

'Sea coral, red wood sorrel and Siberian crabapple.'

I take a sip of the wine, am no connoisseur at all, but this is so good I need to close my eyes when I swallow. The writer downs glass after glass while Papa and I are satisfied with just the one. I've understood that the trick to sitting for a four-hour-long meal without needing to get up to pee is simply to drink as little as possible. I keep an eye on Papa's water glass and my own, and the champagne.

As if the evening was composed just for us, the intermissions are filled with Jewish sounds. Martin Fröst plays his clarinet using his whole body. Like a wild prince he dances between the tables.

The poet and Papa are like day and night. In one way they are so alike, so much their own person, but they are vastly different in attitude. She lays a weary cheek in her hand, says that life is sad and that no one cares when you fall except your family. Papa hardly notices. A photographer comes over to us and wants to take some pictures. The poet and I lean in towards Papa who blows a kiss at the camera. In that moment I feel that the three of us radiate pure joy. The photographer wants another picture, this time only of me. He asks the poet and Papa to lean back a bit. Papa shouts to the photographer:

'You picked the right girl!'

The poet's face darkens.

'That was really rude,' she says and throws her hair back.

When the photographer moves on to other people, I try to explain to her:

'It's just because I'm Izzy's daughter, he wants everybody to see me. That's why he said that.'

'That's just nonsense. It's because he thinks you're younger and more beautiful.'

It almost turns into a fight, wholly improper as the experts on manners and etiquette would say. They might also say the same about Papa's habit of eating with his fingers and the poet's fondness for occasionally taking short naps, fiddling with her phone or messing with the table decorations and her two pairs of glasses. I have no idea what the experts would have thought of the number of glasses of wine consumed by our tablemates.

The poet stands and leaves the table. When she comes back she sits with her eyes closed. Minutes later the conversation is once again friendly. Papa says that he'd love to have her read poetry in his store and that he'd like to take her out for dinner. She answers that she would love to. While Papa is concentrating on his food she turns to me and says:

'That thing before, when I got so angry . . . it's just jealousy really. You see, my father never loved me.'

I want to hug her but I'm not sure she would appreciate the gesture.

When the main course is being served, I overhear the writer talking to someone on the other side of the table.

'Writing about other people is just plain ugly,' he says. 'To lay open the lives of other people, the way Lars Norén does, I don't care how good a playwright he might be.'

I stick my nose in.

'But if someone wants to write a book about their father, should one only write positive things, then?'

The writer gulps another half-glass of that expensive wine and wipes his mouth:

'No, no, children always have that right. They can do exactly what they want.'

The American ambassador steps up to the podium on the Blue Hall's staircase. She reads Dylan's thank-you speech. It's good, it's American, correct, neat and plain. I whisper to the writer that they considered asking me to read the speech. He looks at me and says:

'I think that would have been better.'

He really is a gentleman.

2012

We're in London. Papa will read tonight at a hastily arranged poetry evening at The Dentist, a dental clinic turned cultural venue. Rather than having a nice time together, our weekend is all work and interviews with Papa in the limelight.

We sit in London Fields, an enormous park with thick-trunked trees, lawns and people playing cricket. A collection of poems Papa gathered for the evening is spread across our laps. It's a mix of his own poems, others by Dorothy Parker, Langston Hughes, Patti Smith and Allen Ginsberg. Cuttings he has pasted on to sheets of paper and then photocopied. Comments are scrawled in the margins. He does this in all his books, he pens angry or loving notes directed at the author. He often writes things such as 'So what!' or 'Why did you wait until page 72 instead of saying this on page 1?' If he feels some words have racist implications, he simply crosses them out and writes a biting comment at the side.

Annabel, a potter and a close friend of Papa's who has adopted us here in London, calls me. In eager tones she informs us that Papa's old friend, Lou Killen, has just under-gone an operation at Charing Cross Hospital. She thinks Papa and Lou would both be delighted if they had a chance to meet. I've never heard of the guy, but Annabel tells me that Lou was a key figure in the folk-music movement and that he had a wonderful rowdy voice. She says:

'He must be around seventy-five now.'

I'm holding the telephone, so Papa, who's been listening, screams to make sure that Annabel hears:

'You have to take us there right away!'

A few minutes later Annabel pulls up in her car at the park entrance. We pull out into London traffic and are in no time completely lost. She stops and hurries towards a tiny ice-cream van. Does the man possibly know the way? He offers to lead us there. We zig-zag down tiny alleys behind the ice-cream van until the driver points out our destination. Papa, satisfied, drums his fingers on the glove compartment, bragging:

'Great things are always happening to me!'

At the reception desk Annabel asks for a Mr Lou Killen. The woman behind the desk looks up from her computer screen, shakes her head and says that she has no patient reg-istered with that name.

Annabel insists. She gestures towards Papa:

'They haven't seen each other for forty years. It would be amazing if they could reunite.'

The receptionist searches her register again, hesitates slightly but says:

'Actually, we do have a Louisa Killen ...'

Is there some misunderstanding, perhaps a relative of Lou's who had surgery? Annabel ploughs on.

'Could you phone please and ask if she knows Izzy Young?'

The woman picks up her phone, closes her window, then opens it once again.

'Louisa says that she knows him very well and she'd be overjoyed if you'd come up for a visit.'

We take the lift, unsure who it is we'll be meeting, but the instant we enter the room we understand. She sits on the bed in a long hospital gown and wearing a synthetic wig in a pageboy cut. Her large hands grasp a bag on her lap, her lips painted soft pink. In a high-pitched voice she bursts out:

'Izzy!'

Carefully she stands to be hugged. When they fall into one another's arms the wig slides off kilter and when Papa presses her a little too hard, in a somewhat deeper voice she says, 'Ow!'

Walking with difficulty she leads us to the day room. Everything in there is beige. They sit next to each other, hold hands, immediately begin reminiscing about their New York days. The wig is still crooked but none of us bother to alter it. They're back in the sixties, the concerts, friends and places. Their eyes are shining and they laugh beautifully, the way only old friends can do. Are they avoiding things that might be painful or have they actually landed where they were fifty years ago? They don't mention a single word about the operation Papa's friend has had.

When Louisa waves goodbye at the lift she shouts:

'From now on I'm going to start lecturing about folk music!'

I'm thinking what a brave woman she is.

In the car, on the way to the venue where Papa is reading, he tells us how his friend was a master of seduction and taught Pete Seeger a dozen songs. And then he shouts:

'I can't believe it! How can someone his age have so much hair? Mine started falling out when I was sixteen!'

Late that night Papa reads poetry on an outdoor stage, his bald patch covered by a knitted skullcap. Coloured bulbs light the courtyard and the leaves of the trees cast shadows against the evening sky. The place is sold out and people climb garden walls to see the stage. When Papa gets lost in his jumbled sheets of poems, reading a couple more than once, I gather the courage to join him on stage. I place my chair next to his and point out each poem in turn. My finger finally lands on 'Ku Klux', a poem by Langston Hughes, the poet closest to Papa's heart. He reads quietly, enunciates every syllable describing the evil racist hatred. Rage runs down Papa's cheeks. The courtyard falls silent, the audience and I sit gasping for air.

We drive home in the late night, the low terraced houses of London pass by outside the car's windows as Papa counts pound notes earned that evening. He has a difficult time telling pounds from kronor, is stubborn in the belief that he's been paid too little, still his mood is elevated. I roll down my window. The streetlights are foggy streaks as we speed by and a couple of banknotes escape Papa's fist and flutter inside the car. It feels like a Jim Jarmusch film. We're all high after an enchanted day and evening. Papa's eyes are glowing. Annabel drives, Papa sits beside me in the back, stroking her hair, then kisses me on the cheek shouting:

'Thank you, thank you! Without the two of you this day never could have happened!'

That same summer Nikolai, just turned seven, starts lessons at the outdoor pool at Eriksdalsbadet. It's so cute that Papa has to see it. I organize swimwear, cakes, drinks and sandwiches and pick Papa up from the store. Tiny white clouds frolic over the sky. We've hardly started to move before his hymn to Sweden starts: how he loves the trees, the dark-green foliage, wants to know how long they've been standing there.

We park close to the pool and I'm pleased. Arrived in good time, sun shining. It's the second week of July and most Stockholmers are away on holiday. I push everyone through the revolving gate and Nikolai saunters across the verdant green lawn with his eyes buried in a comic book. There is almost no one here today and Papa exclaims:

'Wow, you'd never find a place like this in America!'

It has probably been many years since he was last at a swimming pool. I get settled on a bench close to the pool and he tells me he'd just like to sit there 'for ever'. Nikolai hops in the water. The shrill voices of the children mix with calm instructions from the swimming teacher. Hands and feet play in the clear blue chlorinated water. Papa isn't lost in a phone or magazine; he just sits and watches his grandson learning to swim. I try to sit as serenely as Papa does. He looks up at me with tears in his eyes:

'Thanks for bringing me.'

I start thinking about all he's taught me about being grateful. How he, when I was little, would count all the things Sweden gave us: free lunches in school, clean streets, summer camp and after-school clubs. Dropping me off at school, he would often comment:

'In America they'd have police standing here with guns.'

He would count the number of students in my class:

'Only twenty-two? In America there'd be at least forty!'

He pointed to signs at the dentist saying that 'Dental care for children is free', said that fixing teeth would cost millions in the States. He pointed at the daycare centres, the green parks. He pointed at practically everything, saying that you'd never find anything like it in the USA. All my life I've heard him say:

'Sweden is fantastic, even if it is only a tiny little duck pond.'

1987

The Jews for Israeli–Palestinian Peace Association has a meeting at the store. A long table is set with coffee and some cookies. Papa is the chairman. I'm bored. The adults babble on while I do my homework. Sometimes I make a few kronor polishing shoes. I take one krona fifty per shoe and it adds up. We're still living in the cellar.

After listening for a couple of hours I raise my hand so that I also can be acknowledged.

'Excuse me . . . but do you really think that you can do something to make peace over there by sitting here and talking? Do you think people in Israel or Palestine care?'

They laugh. I don't know that much about these things, just sit on the sidelines, play with their children in other rooms, observe some Jewish holidays with the association, dunking salad in saltwater to symbolize the tears of slaves, lighting eight candles without really knowing why. We never do these things at home and I've only ever been in the synagogue once. There were guards outside with earpieces and they checked our names off on lists. Papa put a kippa on and I didn't understand any of the songs they were singing. I know that Papa gets angry about the way they divide the men from the women. But we were allowed to sit together. And when everyone sang his eyes filled with tears.

We never talk about Israel and Palestine, about Cambodia, Vietnam or Hitler. He keeps those worlds away from me, or else he's just not interested in sharing. All I know is that things get heated sometimes, like when Papa shook hands with a guy in a funny turban whose name was Arafat. That made some other guy call Papa an anti-Semite on the radio. Papa says that the moment you question something a Jew does you're automatically called an anti-Semite. That hurt him, that unjust accusation by a crazy person on the radio.

When the meeting is over Papa collects the coffee mugs and folds a one-hundred-krona note into his trouser pocket. He gets some money for letting the association meet in the store. Afterwards we walk to Jerusalem Kebab and eat falafel. The walls there are covered with mirrors and posters in another language. You get huge portions and drinks are included. We sit there for a long time before walking back to the store. We are almost friends with the guy who carves the kebab.

2016

The Nobel Banquet is over and we ascend the stone steps
bedecked with flowers. Up on the mezzanine the ball will
be starting and it feels good to stretch our legs after sitting
still for four hours. Looking down over the crowd in the
main hall we spot Patti Smith, who stands out in her black
suit. She's alone. Maybe she's lost, or does she feel embarrassed about messing up the song? I point her out to Papa
but we're both too shy to call out.

There's a live orchestra playing on the balcony and television hosts are dancing in front of the cameras. I take
Papa's hand and pull him out on to the dance floor. No one
dances the way Papa and I do, even if we do it carefully. A
woman, a stranger, invites him to dance but when the song
comes to an end he wobbles and would rather just sit. He
keeps an eye on my handbag, holds it on his knee while I
look for another dance partner. Unfortunately they don't
play any tangos.

Just before midnight he wants to go home. I would have
liked to stay, perhaps attended one of the afterparties, but

his gaze is cloudy, and he never says he wants to go unless he's serious.

We navigate the stairs with care, he holds the flower decorations tight with one hand and grips my arm with the other. Now and then he plucks a leaf or a flower while trying to keep his balance. Below us, the wide hall, built to resemble a plaza, opens up. It's nearly empty now and the lights are dimmed. The candelabras have been extinguished but some flowers, napkins and a few gold coins remain scattered on the tables among the coffee cups. Everything still reeks of elegance. The waiters, all in white, are silently clearing tables. It's like a film from the 1930s. A waitress says we're lovely and asks to take our picture. We smile, genuinely happy with the evening.

When the taxi stops outside my building I see that the bar on the corner is still open. I know the owners and we pop in to show ourselves off. The contrast between our formal wear and how the usual clientele are dressed is priceless. Then we go up to my place, sneaking through the door so as not to wake the family. I kick off my shoes, help Papa brush his teeth and undress. His silk socks are still intact. He's asleep as soon as his head hits the pillow. I turn off the lights, pack up the many items that made up his outfit. Hang my dress again on the bookcase, admire how it secretly glitters in the darkness. It's mine for another few hours, then I'll have to return it.

1987

I am lying in my bed in the cellar, squinting through the darkness at the pipes that crawl across the ceiling. What if someone wants something from their cellar storage in the middle of the night? I don't want them to hear Papa snoring. There's only a door between us and the basement passage. I tiptoe across the floor and poke him hard on the shoulder until he stops, then rush back under my warm covers.

I wonder if we'll ever get our things back, the stuff we had at Kocksgatan. The enforcement authority probably has it, maybe locked up in a warehouse somewhere, or else it's already been mashed up at the rubbish dump. I think about the wooden box with all the pictures of me when I was a baby, and some pictures of my American cousins. I try to remember that black-and-white picture of Mama and Papa when they were kissing. They looked so in love, staring deeply into one another's eyes. Mama had round cheeks and Papa had a beard. The box was painted white and had a red cross on the top. I used to love looking at all the pictures.

A stray sliver of streetlight paints the stairs leading down from the store. I curl up under the blanket, listen to Papa breathing and am almost asleep when someone starts pulling on the outer door. My body stiffens. I hold my breath, my heart beats hard against the bedcovers and I can feel it pounding all the way up in my throat. I try to cry out but can't make a sound. Again the door handle is pushed and pulled up and down, several times. I want to run to Papa but I can't move.

'Papa . . . Papa . . .'

I try to make sounds but all that comes out of my mouth is a thin whisper. He doesn't wake up. I hear a thump, like someone trying to push the door with a shoulder. I manage to sit up. Straight as an arrow. I pull my legs out from under the covers and place them on the stone floor. My legs are shaking, I don't know if it's because I'm afraid or because I'm naked. I'm about to take that first step when I notice the sounds that were so loud a minute ago have suddenly disappeared. There is only some humming inside my ears. I freeze, then press my fingernails into the palms of my hands and try to breathe. One of my legs twitches strangely. I hold a hand over my heart and silently count to ten. Slowly my heartbeat and breath returns. But up in the store it's totally silent.

I bend down, sweep my hand across the floor. Find a T-shirt, hold it in front of my chest and sneak up the stairs. Don't want to wake Papa. If anyone is up there, they aren't moving. I step as quietly as I can, one stair at a time so they don't creak. There are places where the wood is split or nails stick up, but I know where to put my feet. Up in the kitchenette I press myself tightly against the one wall you can't see from the street. Carefully, I peek my head into the store itself. Dark windows. There's no one standing outside the glass door. No one out walking their dog. I run quickly into the middle of the store. For several seconds I can be seen from all the windows with only a T-shirt held in front of me. No, nobody here. Three quick steps and I'm in the kitchenette again. Then quickly downstairs to Papa.

I lie down in bed. Get myself warm. Was it a dream? Did I doze off without realizing it? Or maybe one of Papa's friends was just checking to see that the door was locked. Tomorrow I'll tie a string around Papa's toe, then all I have to do is pull on it if he starts snoring or something else happens.

2017

It's June and Papa phones me from the store. He shouts:

'Everybody gets to go places except for me.'

Now he wants to go on holiday too. At least two weeks. Preferably to New York. I tell him he can't go alone, that he needs to have somebody with him. He seems to agree to this but doesn't understand how much effort it will take for me to make it happen.

A couple of weeks later he's made arrangements to visit a friend in Copenhagen. He bought the train tickets from a tiny travel agency around the corner. At his apartment we pack a suitcase: underwear, shirts, toothbrush and medicines. Before I go home I say:

'I'll take the suitcase with me to my house and I'll pick you up at the store tomorrow. You'll sleep at my house and the next morning I'll take you to the station. Okay?'

He nods, but his eyes say something different.

'Papa, you don't need to think about anything, I'll call and remind you.'

This has become one of my standard phrases. It usually works; he relaxes when I relieve him of responsibility.

The next day he stands ready at the door when I come to pick him up; nicely dressed, freshly shaved, but with a suitcase I don't recognize in his hand.

'Papa, we already packed a suitcase yesterday with everything you need. It's at my house.'

He laughs and says 'All right' when I suggest we leave this second suitcase in the store. I drive him back to my place and after dinner he sleeps soundly on the sofa.

I'm tiptoeing silently around the kitchen the next morning when I hear him roar:

'Good morning! I feel like a newborn baby. I had such a fantastic trip!'

I look out from the kitchen. He's still lying under the covers.

'But, Papa ... you haven't left yet.'

He laughs.

A little while later we're eating porridge and sandwiches and drinking coffee when he tells me:

'That train ride was a piece of cake!'

'Papa, you haven't gone yet ...'

He looks at me surprised and asks:

'Am I going crazy?'

A few minutes later we're in the lift, finally on our way to Central Station. He examines his suitcase, lifts it up and down several times with his right hand to check the weight.

'Wow. It's heavier now than when I left!'

'We're on the way to the station, Papa. You haven't left yet.'

We pass between splashes of morning sun and shadow. He chuckles, pokes me playfully in the side as we walk towards the bus stop. This is what I love; our ability to laugh, no matter what is happening.

Forty-five minutes later I've seated him on the train, with a sign hanging around his neck. It says: 'My name is Izzy Young. I'm on my way to Copenhagen'. Further down I've printed my telephone number and the name of the person meeting him when he arrives. I ask the passengers sitting closest to him to make sure he doesn't get off the train before it gets to the last stop. They seem helpful. I kiss him on the forehead and put the bag from 7-Eleven, with sandwiches and a soft drink, in his lap. His trousers are clean. I step back into summer on the platform. Wave through the train window, just as we've always done. I wonder what the other people in the carriage think. About me. The whole way home I'm repeating the same mantra in my head: *Please let him arrive safely. Please let him remember his suitcase.*

During the week that follows I'm in daily contact with the friend he's staying with in Copenhagen. She says it's a lot more work than she expected and that she forces him to take a siesta, even if he protests. If nothing else she can get a rest then. She makes sure he drinks plenty of water and reminds him often to go to the toilet. The rest of the time they drink coffee with friends or enjoy nature from a folding deck chair. This is not the kind of activity that Papa usually likes, but now he seems satisfied.

Seven days later he arrives back. I meet him on the station platform and find him in one piece, clean and lightly tanned. He holds the suitcase in his hand, says the trip 'wasn't that exciting'. But his face is rested and he looks handsome. He wants to go to the store immediately to check the post and see what's been happening, and believe it or not, he doesn't have time for coffee.

1987

The streetlights in Högdalen cast shadows on Papa's back. He walks in front of me, an oblong shadow trailing behind him. He's wound a plastic bag with groceries around his wrist and his hand is red from the cold. He has a stomach bug, threw up on the metro a few minutes ago. Now he bends over the snow again. I drop further behind, kick at clumps of ice, look in the other direction. I don't want to see Papa's vomit and I don't want to go to the dingy apartment that we're now staying at for a month. This one is on the ground floor. Cars rush by the window.

There's nothing there except two mattresses, a kitchen table and a television. If you want to watch TV you have to take a chair from the kitchen. We don't usually talk when we eat there and it echoes when we put down our knives and forks. We'll move back to the store soon. That will be better.

Cars zoom past the two of us. He is still retching but there's nothing coming up. I stare at the ground, pretending I don't have anything to do with him. He stands and turns towards me. His eyes are black.

'Are you ashamed of me?' he shouts and shakes his fist.

Then he walks away. Silent. Angry. I don't know whether to catch up with him or not.

Three years later we get a real home. Well, not exactly. Mama has had enough of me and Papa moving from one place to another, no fixed address. She's been moving too but does it in a more organized way. She lives and works at different conference centres or even ashrams. Sometimes in Sweden, sometimes in France. She is a cook, an artist, does yoga and meditates. She often sends letters or cassettes she's recorded of herself. The sound is distorted when she breathes too close to the microphone. As I listen to them I start to cry immediately. I visit her in Älmhult, Borlänge, Hedemora and Järna. When she lives in France I can't visit; it's too far away.

But she has an apartment. A three-bedroom apartment in Farsta Strand. I lived there with her a few years ago. Now I move there with Papa. To my place, my Mama-apartment but without my mama. The entrance to our building has some graffiti on it. It also smells kind of strange. But once inside, the orange walls are warm and some of Mama's paintings and books are still there. She left a pack of Tarot cards as well with only pictures of women. I like to lay them out and read them. We live there for a few years, me and Papa. Settled. We rent out one room to different people so we can afford the bills.

2017

'Mind the doors please, the doors are closing.' I'm sitting in a metro carriage when my phone pings. It's a man from England who's writing a book about Papa. He's been in touch with the Library of Congress and he's there reading through Papa's journals that are now in their archives. Would I like to read them too? He sends me a PDF. On the first page I see a scanned image with the words 'Composition Notebook' printed on the blue cover. Papa has written 'June 1985' on it. It looks just like the composition books we had in middle school. I scroll down, reading Papa's minuscule handwriting. He's describing our journey to Jokkmokk, on the night train, how I as a child then asked to sleep high up in the third bed. 'Please, Papa, can I be highest?' He writes:

> She's up there sitting, thinking, reading, rather like a little monkey. She reads a lot of *Starlet* magazines, cramming her head as much as possible with all that lying shit. I'll ask her why she reads it so intensely.

I smile, we share the same memories. I scroll down a bit more. He describes the few hours we spend in Tårrajaur the next morning. We're changing trains. We listen to a boys' choir singing in a church and we grab a snack at a café before killing the last hour in the local library. Papa writes:

> She uses my body as some kind of couch – as if it's just there to use. And it's okay. It is part of our time together on this earth. We should not live to become memories – but how can one always avoid such thoughts.
>
> Now we are in a quiet library, and Philomène leaves me to read her books as I write. It is part of the agreement between us.

Suddenly I'm caught short of breath. Everyone. Anyone at all can from this day forward read Papa's journals. They're out there, perhaps they'll all be put online. What else has he written? Can I change my mind, ask for them back? I send a message to the writer and beg him to let me know if he finds details that are too private. He's already scanned and sent a whole journal but I don't have the energy to read it. All my life I've been surrounded by Papa's words: in his newsletter, journals, letters and poems. Long monologues sometimes where I'd wait for ever before I could hear my own voice. I haven't even read his autobiography. His words have taken up so much space that I've almost developed an allergy to reading anything more by him or about him. But when it comes like this, in small doses and so full of love and affection, I lay my head on my desk and start to cry. As self-centred as he is, he has managed to see me.

1988

I've spent a night at a friend's. One who lives in a house. A minute ago her mother sat by the table brushing some mascara on. She got black on her eyelids and some under an eye. She didn't care, just wiped the worst of it away with spit on a piece of paper towel. Then she rushed off to work taking my friend's little sister with her. It's quiet in the house now. My friend goes to the toilet. When I hear the door lock, I start looking through the cupboards and the fridge. I scan the shelves. Take a tin of tuna and stuff it in the bottom of my school bag. All my movements are rapid, jerky; I have to do this quickly before she flushes and comes back. Then I pretend like I'm breathing normally and say I need to go home and study.

I always notice friends' fridges. They're stuffed full, loaded: eggs, yoghurt, juice, meat, fish, chunks of Parmesan cheese and jars of sun-dried tomatoes. In the cupboards they have chocolate, crisps and dried fruit in plastic bags closed with pink plastic clips. They have cornflakes, flour and sugar all in tightly closed containers.

One of Papa's friends works at a conference centre, in a kitchen painted in soft pastel colours. It's outside of town and she said I could come and visit. I go, thinking perhaps I might be able to do my ninth-grade work-experience weeks there. Dinner has already been served and all the tables wiped clean. She asks about me and Papa. When she manages to coax an admission that we have too little she begins filling two paper bags. Milk, flour, rice, salt, a large lump of cheese, a bar of soap, plastic gloves, light bulbs, a cooking pot and a packet of batteries. They are packed with determined hands when the lights are turned out. I haul the bags to the bus stop, careful not to let the bottoms drag on the pavement. A pullover lies on top of each bag so that no one from her job could see the contraband I'm carrying home to Stockholm. I take a bus and then the commuter train, drag myself up the steep hills in Farsta. Finally I can unload the goods on to the shelves in our pantry. Papa looks on, curious, but doesn't say much. This is natural for him; almost everything he owns has come as a gift. In one single night we devour the whole cheese.

2018

I see him the same instant I step out on the stage. He's sitting in the audience, as enthusiastic as the thousand children that fill the Concert Hall. He missed the opening show because he forgot about it. But he's here now. Lasse and the children picked him up. Anytime I'm on stage I know immediately where he's sitting. I'm playing a girl in outer space, and as I look out over the audience I see the spotlights reflecting in his glasses. He's smaller now but he still stands out clearly. Papa is here, my children are here, Lasse and some of my friends are here.

After the show Papa pushes his way to the stage. Crying huge tears. We hold hands and he whispers:

'You're amazing. Nobody can do it the way you do.'

A friend takes a picture, preserving the moment for ever, our hands entwined. Papa is laughing one minute and crying the next. It doesn't feel fair to take his picture given the state he's in.

Later that evening I look at the picture again. Thinking that we're so beautiful I put the picture up on Facebook.

The likes start pouring in. I didn't even tag his name, but a picture of Papa always gets at least a hundred thumbs-up. Before he falls asleep on the sofa he tells me that this will be the start of something new for me. I don't know, I'm just happy that so many children journeyed with me into outer space, that they were able to sing with a symphony orchestra. I'm happy that he's sleeping on my sofa, that he was around to see this performance too.

2018

Bob Dylan is playing at Stockholm Waterfront, a venue in town. We've seen him many times before but for me this feels like the first time ever. He gives a lot, seems to be at one with his band. Usually he stands as if he's hiding and it's hard to tell what song he's playing as they all sound identical. But now he stands firm, feet apart, a hand on his waist and large hat on his head. His voice comes from within. From the very first number I can sense that he's got the feeling. After a while Papa turns to me and asks who's on stage. I whisper:

'Bob Dylan.'

He looks at me in shock, points:

'That's Bob Dylan?'

'Yes . . .'

'He's incredible.'

'Yes, Papa, he is.'

We listen intensely. Small lamps with copper threads light the band from above. Dylan sings into an old-fashioned microphone, shuffles across the stage as if he were wearing slippers. It's only when you see him moving that you first understand how old he is.

Papa holds my hand. Tonight his hands are warm. Clean. He whispers:

'You could never do it like this in America.'

I look at him:

'But, Daddy, they're all Americans, every one of them.'

He hears what I say, nods, listens to the music. I sit next to my father, watch the tears roll down his cheek as he mumbles again and again:

'It's just so fucking beautiful.'

After the concert the Dylan nerds want Papa to autograph their tickets. They call out 'Izzy! Izzy!', wondering what Papa thought about the show. They say they have every record Dylan ever made, describing in metres the size of their stacks, saying they've seen him play here, seen that concert there. Papa laughs, promises he'll send them something special, that he'll make copies of stuff he has in the store. I drag him by the sleeve to get him out of there.

We get home and in no time he's sleeping like a baby, snoring and talking sweetly in his sleep. Lasse's in the kitchen. We laugh when I replay the conversation Papa and I had during the concert. It feels good, Papa and the kids asleep, most of my family gathered together.

The next morning Papa jerks awake and shouts loudly from the sofa:

'What a concert! Fantastic! Dylan was better than ever!'

And Papa remembers everything. Exactly. He's ready for

the day, punches the air, can't find one shoe, is in a hurry and wants to walk all the way to the store by himself. I let him. He wears Lasse's jacket, because of course he forgot to bring one of his own, in spite of the frost sparkling on Stockholm's pavements.

2018

Today Papa said that he wants to be cremated. He said that he doesn't care that it's not the Jewish tradition. I asked him where he wants his ashes spread.

'I don't know . . . anywhere.'

'But I do want a place where I can go, to remember you and be with you.'

'You'll always be able to find me,' he says, making circles in the air with his arm.

'Mariatorget maybe?'

He nods. That's how simply this subject passes as we cut through the graveyard on the way to the health clinic. The sun beams through February's bare branches and Papa complains that the church across the street looks too 'bright' since they repainted it.

1989

When I get home from school Papa is standing by the cooker. Yesterday I yelled at him because our toilet is always so disgusting, with pee on the rim and on the floor. He's boiling water in the big pan, the one we use when we cook pasta. The windows are all steamed up and sweat is running down Papa's forehead. Half the toilet seat is sticking up out of the pasta pan. He smiles wide and scrubs the toilet seat with the brush we use for dishes.

'You see? I always listen to you!'

He's proud, now he's doing the right thing, what I asked for. All I can do is stare.

Often it's me shouting, then he shrinks and nods. Maybe he feels shame somehow; in his world I'm always right. But he still decides when I should be home in the evening. I have to be home from the teen club in Farsta at eleven o'clock, even though all the other kids go home at midnight after the film has finished. I have to keep track of time in the cinema's darkness, ride the metro by myself. I walk the last bit home in the middle of the street. That's what Mama taught me. If you are lit by streetlights there is less risk of being raped. Papa doesn't understand that it's more dangerous to walk home alone than with the others. But I do as he says. Papa is still the one who makes the rules.

When I get home he's sitting at the kitchen table in a T-shirt and boxer shorts. He's playing solitaire. There's no limit to the number of times he can lay the cards. His watch lies on the table next to him. Ever since I can remember he's been extremely strict about being on time. He usually taps the glass on the face of his watch if I'm even a minute late or if anyone else is.

Last week a friend of his gave us an old television, but now Papa has thrown it out because he thought we were turning into idiots, staring at it all the time. I agree with him a little. I got hooked on some series they were showing on a cable channel. I don't understand how we could watch it without paying.

When Papa is home he is almost always sleeping. I'm the only one who cares about the place being nice. He hasn't put up a single shelf. I did it when I was thirteen. I'm tired of doing everything. And I'm worried because I've seen that Papa's had letters from collection agencies. I opened one, though I know I wasn't supposed to. It was from the energy company and said that Papa hadn't paid. Now he'll have to pay extra. I'm scared that they'll come and take this apartment from us too.

2018

It's nine in the evening and I've just put Natasha to bed, closing her door in order not to wake her. A number I don't recognize rings. I answer in a whisper:

'Hello?'

On the other end there's a friendly female voice:

'Hi, am I speaking to Izzy Young's daughter?'

'Yes . . .'

'I'm a security officer for Stockholm City Transport and we found your father on the platform at Mariatorget Station. He's been wandering back and forth for a while now saying he has a store just around the corner. We understand that this isn't true, but we saw your phone number on the lanyard around his neck.'

I say that he's telling the truth about the store but that it's odd that he's wandering around on the platform. I give her the store's address.

'We'll walk him over,' she says, 'and I'll phone you when we get there.'

She hangs up and I stand still, trying to take it in. Papa is lost. At Mariatorget.

A few minutes later another call from the same number. They're at the store and this time it's Papa's voice I hear. He says he wants to sleep in the store. I say I understand.

A couple of weeks later I call the store at five in the evening and ask him how he's doing. He says 'good'. Then he tells me that he's not crazy but today he's not sure where he lives. He asks if I could tell him the address, just like he did yesterday, just like he did the day before. And just like always my stomach cramps. How will it go today? Natasha is pulling at the leg of my trousers, gestures that she needs help with a game on her iPad. I push her away and she stomps on heavy feet, yelling:

'Aaaarghhhh! Why do you always have to be on the phone?'

She slams the kitchen door so hard the windows rattle.

'Papa, wait there, I'll call a taxi.'

We hang up. I focus on ordering a taxi and then ring the store again.

'Papa, the taxi will be there in an hour. At exactly ten-past six.'

'What? When?'

'You don't have to do anything. I'll call you ten minutes before the taxi comes. Just stay right where you are.'

He promises not to move an inch from his chair.

I set the alarm on my phone so that I won't forget to call back. I then help Natasha with her computer game and start making dinner. Ten minutes before the taxi is due the alarm goes off. I call him just as we're sitting down to eat. He doesn't answer. Has he been standing out in the street waiting since we spoke nearly an hour ago? The thermometer shows it's minus nine degrees. There isn't anything more I can do. I put the phone down next to my plate and start eating. I try my best but I'm unable to follow the dinner conversation. I nod without hearing, chew without tasting, see how beautiful my family is without being there with them. I am constantly checking my phone.

Eighteen minutes later there's a call from a number I don't recognize. I get tunnel vision, stumble out into the living room. A man's voice:

'This is the taxi service. Are you Israel Young?'

'No, I'm his daughter. Did you just get there? I booked the taxi for ten-past six. Can't you see him out there on the pavement?'

'No ...'

'He has grey hair. He's almost ninety.'

'That old!' the driver remarks, smacking his lips, impressed.

'Yes. That's why I ordered a taxi and that's why it's important that you get there on time. Especially now when it's so cold outside.'

'Yeah, well, you know ...'

'He should be wearing a green down jacket.'

'Yeah. Okay. I see him now!'

Papa is located. The taxi doors slam. I can see out the

window again, see the neighbour's windows all lit up, hear my children's voices and I hear Papa shouting:

'Where are you taking me?'

I ask the driver to hand the phone to Papa so that I can talk to him. I try to calm him, try to help him find the taxi card he carries around his neck on the lanyard where his keys are hung. The driver comes on again, telling me that the keys are there but no senior-citizen subsidy card:

'I'm sorry, miss, without the card I can't drive him . . .'

'Please, can't you just look in his pockets?'

'No, I'm not allowed to do that.'

Papa has to go back to the store. Lasse and the children are eating. I count to sixty and call again:

'Papa, I'll be right there. Promise you'll stay in the store!'

In my ugliest sweatpants I hurry out to the car. The cold air cuts right through the fabric. It would be nice if Lasse, for once, would jump to the rescue instead of me. He takes care of the kids, believes he does what he can. But I'm all alone with the stress. We take turns to walk Natasha to daycare in the morning and pick her up in the afternoon, but in addition to that I have a grown-up baby to take care of. I was so distraught the other day over Lasse's inability to understand that I smashed some of our nicest plates on the kitchen floor. He told me I was sick in the head and took the children out. I thank God that Papa's friends help me almost daily.

I drive as fast as I can but force myself to obey red lights. I arrive at the store, drive up on the pavement, right to the door. Papa sits in his chair with his jacket on. A neighbour is keeping him company and they munch ginger snaps left over from Christmas. It seems like they're having a nice time.

'Hi, Papa. I'm driving you home now.'

'Where?' he asks.

When I lock up the store with my own key he points at me and laughs, turns to his friendly neighbour:

'Look! She doesn't trust her father!'

I wrangle his stiff legs into the car. Snow mixed with rain lashes the windscreen, the wipers beat a wild defence and the car glides down the hill.

'Papa, this can't go on. I have to find a home for you now. You don't remember where you live and you can't even take a taxi by yourself.'

He tells me it's never happened before.

'It has, Papa, every day for the last two weeks.'

He is silent for a second before his face lights up with a smile again:

'So then I'll live closer to the store!'

I don't know what to answer, have no idea where he might be able to move to. He is quiet for a minute or so, then mumbles:

'But I'll still have the store though?'

'Yes, I think so . . .'

I'm in the starting gate, getting myself ready. Another marathon I'll have to run. My body tenses, anticipating all the closed doors I'll have to force open. I claw the sheets the second I open my eyes in the morning. No matter what time of day or night it is I'm talking in my head with a social worker or composing an application for elderly housing. Every morning when I open my eyes I feel like I'm running. I'm galloping. In every direction. All at the same time.

1989

I'm in ninth grade and I don't know who to be friends with.
At lunchtime I hide in the woods. I weep in secret when
the school day is finally over and I ride the metro to Papa
and the store. He makes coffee, talks and talks and talks,
shows how brilliant the next issue of his newsletter is going
to be. Pictures and advertisements lay cut up and sorted into
plastic folders. There's a folder for every county in Sweden
taped on the wall. He doesn't see my red eyes. I tell him
he's both blind and deaf, that he doesn't care, that he's just
a stupid idiot. He says sorry:

'Come, let's sit by the window.'

He pats the seat next to him on the Karl Johan sofa, wants
us to look deeply into each other's eyes. He wants me to tell
him everything I feel. Silence. I stare at my hands. When
I look up I can see him writing in his head. Frantically.
He's busy. He's nursing a poem, is filled with this unique
moment unfolding between father and daughter. I disappear. Tell him nothing about school. Drink tea from a dirty
mug that tastes like coffee.

2018

Nikolai and I are swinging in the evening twilight. Fairy lights illuminate the bar in the park. We sit close together on the big swing and he swings so high that I almost fall off. He shows me how far he can jump and my heart overflows with love. We draw a line in the dirt after every hop. He's both big and little. How many more evenings like this will we have?

When we come home, shutting the front door, Papa, who was sleeping on the sofa, wakes. His wide-open eyes glisten in the dark room. He calls out:

'What? Does everybody live here now?'

I sit down on the edge of the sofa and pat his arm.

'Papa, you're at my place.'

'What?'

'In my apartment. At Philomène's.'

His eyes stare, questioning, but he seems secure enough with my arm resting on his. I tell him that I picked him up from the store, how he's eaten dinner with us, sat on the balcony for a while wrapped up in a blanket and how after that he watched some silly film with the kids.

'But how did I get here? Is this my room?'

'No, Papa. We're at my place now. Shall I put the light on?'

I switch on the ceiling light, a five-armed fixture from the forties. He points:

'So that's not my light?'

'No, it's mine.'

'But this is my bed!'

'No. It's our sofa. You usually sleep on it.'

He looks over the room. I say that we can walk around so that he can get his bearings. I tense my stomach muscles so that I can help him up without straining my back. He thinks we're at his place, even when he sees Natasha sleeping in the big bed and Nikolai waving from his bedroom. He wants me to open the curtains so that he can look outside. When I do, he sees trees. He sees trees from his own windows too. Finally he asks to see the kitchen. Drunk with sleep he shuffles forward carefully with me holding him under the arm. I recognize what he's feeling, that sense of being in a misty dream together.

He stops in front of the fridge, runs his fingers over the door, over photos and drawings held in place with magnets. He says he wants to look inside.

'This is my fridge,' I say, opening it.

We look inside. It's full. A pizza box lays at a slant across everything else thrown haphazardly inside. He nods:

'You're right. This isn't my fridge.'

I lead him back to the sofa. He jokes:

'Promise you won't call the newspapers. Don't tell anyone.'

I tease him saying I *won't* promise anything. I drape the blanket around his shoulders, brush the hair from his eyes:

'Sleep now, Papa. In the morning you'll probably know where you are.'

2018

The church bells in Vitabergsparken are chiming ten o'clock when I broach the subject. He's been sitting on the sofa, waiting while I took Natasha to pre-school. He's folded the sheet and blanket in a tidy pile next to him. The grey light of winter filters through the windows. He's hunched slightly towards his right side, leaning against the cushions. I sit across from him in an armchair, dare to look him right in the eyes:

'Papa, we're going to have to close the store.'

'Close the store!'

I explain how much the rent is, I remind him how many times he's got lost. I say it again, this time very clearly:

'We have to close the store.'

He laughs:

'You keep saying "we".'

He doesn't understand how many friends pitch in to keep his store alive. They take care of nearly everything when there's a concert and help me by putting him in a taxi at the end of each day. I repeat it all ten times. Try to find words that won't hurt. He mumbles:

'I'll have to be better.'

'You can't help this. It's amazing that you've been able to run the store this long; most men die when they're around eighty. You're almost ninety now and stronger than most people. But you have Alzheimer's and you can't get the help that you need as long as you keep the store.'

'Why hasn't anybody told me!' he shouts when I mention his illness. 'Isn't there a flyer, something I can read?'

I sit next to him, take his hand. In the street below cars and an ambulance pass. He insists that his body is strong and that he takes good care of the store.

'It isn't even messy there,' he says, frowning with disbelief.

We walk out into the hall. His belt is broken so we'll have to get him a new one. I help him put his down jacket on, zip it for him, struggle to get his winter boots on, with ice studs to keep him from slipping. He's cut his socks because they were too tight around his calves. Pieces of fabric now hang like tongues around his ankles.

Outside we take tiny steps towards the bus that will take us the short distance to the shopping centre. He is afraid of slipping and lets the first bus drive off right in front of us. With pride he tells me that he never runs these days. The bus-stop display says it's nine minutes until the next bus. I consider walking instead, it isn't far at all, but Papa would rather sit on the bench. His upper body leans heavily to one side. I look at my watch. It's already quarter-past eleven. Half the day is gone. Shouldn't inner-city buses run more often? I stare at my phone, try to answer a message about a job while Papa points to something he sees on the ground that he wants me to investigate. I turn away from him, groaning with irritation. He gives up, quietly watches the cars pass. He's really leaning too much. Should I call the health information hotline?

Nine minutes later we sit on the bus, face to face on seats for disabled people. He fixes me with a curious look, his yellow knitted hat glowing like neon. I can't help smiling back at him. On the short ride to Skanstull I manage to say:

'If we close the store, we'll have more time for each other. We can go to the cinema and discover new cafés. Maybe take a trip somewhere. I think Croatia might be nice!'

His eyes sparkle and he smiles, as if he were hearing a story told by Santa Claus. I want to hold his hands. I want to tell him I was being harsh and unfair.

The door hisses open and I help my crooked father down the steps. A cold wind and an icy drizzle lash us. I grab the arm of his jacket:

'Papa, I need a hug.'

In the middle of that crowd getting on and off the bus he pulls me in close and holds me:

'Oh, baby ...'

He strokes my hair, the green of his down jacket blends with the blue of my own. I cry against his shoulder:

'Papa, please, please close the store.'

He hushes, pats, says he won't go against me. I dry my tears on my sleeve:

'I love the store too.'

'I know,' he says. 'We'll find other things to do.'

It's good hearing him say those words, though I know they'll all be forgotten in an instant. We walk towards the shopping centre. I'm not sure if he is holding on to me or if I'm almost carrying him because he's leaning an awful lot. But it's warm between our jackets.

The lady standing in the entrance selling the *Big Issue* watches us. I stare at the ground, start to cry again, because she sees us, because her gaze was friendly. Compassionate. We pass by without buying a magazine, shuffle through the doors and into the enchantment of music and consumer goods. Our jackets move apart. Papa stops in front of signs, reads out load, sounding each syllable. Warm air blows from the entrances to all the stores and I want to stay here with Papa for hours, looking at stuff, gliding from shop to shop, stopping for coffee and cake in the new food court. But I need to look for work. The entire morning is almost gone.

We leave the shops, Papa wearing the new belt we bought. He wants to go to the store right away. He wants to take the metro, refuses to go by taxi. At the ticket booth I tell the woman that I'm his guide, so I don't have to pay. He holds up a key instead of his metro card at the turnstile. The woman opens the gate from inside the booth. When we've passed through, Papa turns to me and whispers:

'Did you see how I did that? Pretended to be an old man?' He laughs. 'We make a good team, you and me!'

We take the lift to the platform. Now he's leaning so much I can clearly feel his weight against me. I tell him this, asking again if he's certain he wants to take the metro. He says that he's only leaning because we're holding hands.

On the platform I explain to him how to get to the store:

'You take the train two stations to Slussen and then change to the red line.'

'Of course,' he says, but his eyes shift uncertainly when the train arrives.

He steps on to the train. Should I get on with him? I look up at the platform clock. A man on the train calls:

'Izzy!'

I recognize him from the corner stationery store where Papa always buys his office supplies. The man seems immediately to grasp the situation; he takes Papa by the arm and winks at me as if to say, 'It's fine. I got this. Go on now.' Papa lets the man lead him to a place where they can stand comfortably. I'm so relieved I turn immediately and walk back up to the turnstiles. Perhaps I'll manage to look for some work today after all. But when I hear the swoosh from the train as it leaves the platform, my stomach clenches. I'm sure. I'm absolutely sure. He won't find his way to the store.

2018

My good friend has put a glass of red wine on the table in front of me. She knows that I hardly ever drink. I'm chopping lettuce while she's frying onions. My voice has gone up a notch while hers has dropped a little. Our children run in and out of the kitchen, snatching a leaf or a piece of freshly sliced cucumber. They can probably feel the air of irritation in the room. My friend stirs a tin of chopped tomatoes into the pan.

'I can't understand how you can give so much time to your father. Aren't you overdoing it a bit? I think you're doing more than you really need to.'

I say nothing, go on chopping lettuce.

'It isn't normal. I think you need to do other things too.' She stirs the sauce.

I'm thinking that she says this because we don't see each other very often. Maybe because she was never that close to her father. Or because her parents are younger, stronger, can take care of themselves. Maybe she says it because her father didn't always put her first.

I swallow, stare down at my fingers. Tiny salad leaves are pasted to my pale skin. Again she starts questioning the things I do for Papa and says that she would have 'thrown in the towel a long time ago'. Finally I slam the table hard with my open hand. Drops of wine splash on to the table-cloth. I boil over, want to grab my kids, throw our jackets out into the hallway. I can feel how my face is turning red as I scream:

'Come on, kids, let's go! This is no place to be.'

But I don't. My knees just shake and my hand lies numb on the table after that slap. She says she's sorry, turns the cooker off, sits beside me.

'I care about you, that's all.'

She touches my cheek. I nod and tears fall, though I don't want to be stuck in her hug. I see everything from the outside, thinking that she doesn't understand, doesn't want to, can't. She sees herself as the adult and me as the child.

1991

It's Saturday morning and I laze between warm sheets hearing Mama and Papa talking in the kitchen. Mama got a job in Stockholm a while ago and moved back to Farsta. We each have our own room now: Mama, Papa and me. They live together as friends. I don't think Mama really wants to live with him; she's probably doing it to be nice. In many ways she's incredibly loyal to those she once loved. Or maybe she's doing it for my sake?

It smells of fried onions and fresh coffee. I can hear that they don't agree, but they still want to keep discussing whatever it is. Is it politics, or a poem that's got under their skin? Papa has slid a note under my door. I tiptoe over and read: 'Good morning. Come out when you're hungry! Today's menu: scrambled eggs, smoked salmon, melon and apple juice.'

I go out to the kitchen. Papa stands at the cooker slicing mushrooms to fry with the eggs. On the kitchen table Mama has arranged the haul from her morning walk: knotty branches, feathers, a bird skeleton, some moss.

Almost everything she touches turns into something wild and exciting.

Somehow it works. I'm sitting here naked under my dressing gown, perspiring slightly. I'm both child and grown-up. Enjoying being with them while feeling at the same time that the three of us together is very strange.

2018

Papa has a fever, thirty-nine degrees, is lying on our sofa. I cover him with thin sheets and open the window. Maybe if I let fresh air in I can keep the rest of us from catching it. He wants to go to the toilet, constantly. He pees and pees. He pees on the rim. Pees on the floor. I wipe it up, start getting irritated. He wakes up from a short nap, worrying about a concert that doesn't exist. Going on about bookings and jabbering letters. Getting stuck and stuttering:

'P ... P ... P ...'

I don't understand. He yells at me even though Natasha is sleeping:

'Don't you get it? I need to get hold of all of them, not just the ones starting with the letter P!'

And then he wants to pee again. The bathroom is occupied. Nikolai shouts through the door that he has a bad stomach. Papa waits in the kitchen. He's got the chills and his bare legs are shaking. Natasha wakes up, comes out of her room and seeing her grandpa standing in a nappy says:

'Ooooh, he's so cuuuuute.'

Lasse leads her back to bed. Papa wants to pee in the sink. I say that he can't. He begs me to let him pee out on the balcony.

'What is he doing in there?' he shouts at the bathroom door. I get the bucket. Papa grabs hold of the kitchen table with one hand and pulls his nappy down with the other. I hold the bucket, not knowing where to look but wanting to make sure that he doesn't pee all over the floor. He stumbles back towards the sofa. I shout to Nikolai:

'We fixed it. Grandpa peed in the bucket. You don't have to hurry!'

Papa's most important possessions lie on the coffee table: glasses, comb, taxi card and keys. He jangles them in the dark. I ask if he wants me to put the light on. He wants me to, but I decide that it's not a good idea. It's after eleven already. Again he starts going on about that concert, that three hundred people will be turning up:

'Do I have to cancel it?'

'Papa, these days you only put on concerts in the store. There are usually not more than forty people. There aren't any lists. Your next concert is a week from now. You don't need to start thinking about it yet.'

I hear Nikolai flush, want to say goodnight before he falls asleep. Papa has my arm in a vice:

'You have to tell me what to do!'

I raise my voice:

'If you don't stop going on about that damn concert I'll drive you home. I'm serious!'

He folds his arms over his chest like a pouting child:

'No, I want to sleep here.'

He's quiet for a few seconds, then it starts again. Rattling the keys, asking what he's supposed to do, throwing his dentures on the floor. Lasse comes out of the bedroom and whispers:

'Shouldn't you give him a sleeping pill?'

Pill and water are presented in the dark. Papa swallows. I think this is probably what they do in retirement homes. Give them sleeping pills when the staff can't take any more. Or maybe that's part of their daily routine? I've never given him a sleeping pill or ever seen him take one. It takes a few minutes to kick in. I take his temperature in his ear. Still thirty-nine. He wants me to do the other ear too. He puts his glasses under the pillow, says that they should stay there so he doesn't lose them. My hands are shaking:

'No. You'll just break them. Go to sleep!'

I retreat to the kitchen. Lasse follows, holds me in his arms. I take comfort from a slice of white bread with a lot of butter, calm down.

It's almost midnight. We brush our teeth. From our bed we hear him fiddling with his stuff on the table. Despite the fever, despite the pill, he's still awake. I'm reminded of an anecdote he tells often and with pride, about the doctor who couldn't knock him out when he was a child and was about to have an operation. The doctor had to count to one hundred before Papa fell asleep, while most kids were knocked out before the doctor got to ten. I grab my earplugs and say:

'Hope he doesn't pee on the sofa.'

Lasse answers:

'Don't worry, he's got the nappy on.'

Next morning everything is drenched. Sofa, carpet, floor. Papa's nappy, dry as a bone, lies folded on the coffee table. I call a taxi. It's coming in forty-five minutes. I serve scrambled eggs and make toast. He doesn't say he's sorry, just quietly fiddles with stuff on the coffee table.

Outside it's raining constantly. The taxi comes on time. I give the driver a note on which I've written the key code to the building entrance in Fredhäll, ask him to make sure Papa gets into the building. I fasten Papa's seatbelt. Stand outside in my nightdress and raincoat. It's seven degrees outside and I'm relieved and frightened as I watch him drive away.

2018

The synagogue's answering machine asks me to leave
a message:

'Yes, hello. I have a father who is ... Jewish ... he is
almost ninety years old and I'm starting to think about his
funeral, which probably will be ... sometime in the next
few years ... I wonder if there is someone I could talk to and
ask some questions? I don't really know how Jewish funerals
are done ... uhm ... so if you could call me at this number.
But most of all I would like to meet someone in person.
Thank you very much ... have a nice day. Goodbye.'

2018

Umbrella in one hand, pushchair in the other, I struggle up the steep path in Vitabergsparken. Natasha is in the push-chair with her raincoat on backwards and her teddy bear in the hood hanging down on her chest. Rainwater runs in rivers on either side of the path. Soon I'll be going to the synagogue. To meet the woman with the friendly voice who called me on the phone. She coordinates everything that has to do with funerals, explained that our meeting could get cancelled at short notice because she might have to manage someone's funeral urgently as the time period between death and burial is so short. She seemed pleasant. Normal. Not at all ultra-religious or anything like that.

While pushing Natasha up the hill I start thinking about what she said regarding not usually having music at Jewish burials, 'Though some rabbis might allow a little music at the beginning or end of the service.' Papa's whole life has been music. How could it end without it? I've always imagined that the Steamboat Entertainers would play.

Thirty minutes later, Natasha dropped off at pre-school,

I'm at the synagogue near Kungsträdgården. A guard allows me to enter. He tells me to take the lift upstairs, turn right and then left. I try to look harmless. I don't want anyone to think I'm a terrorist.

After getting lost in the hallway I find the office with her name tag. The door is open and she's standing by her desk, speaking on the phone in English. I understand that she's arranging a flight for a body being sent to Israel. Her fingers tap the keyboard while she presses the receiver between her cheek and shoulder. A shawl is wrapped around her head. When she sees me she waves. Not wanting to interrupt, I quietly pull my wet boots off and place them and my umbrella outside the door. Further down the hall I spy a small kitchen and take the liberty of going in there. I fill a kettle and make tea for both of us.

Minutes later she's in the kitchen, apologizing for keeping me waiting:

'I love that you're making yourself at home! I haven't had any breakfast. Care to join me?'

We sit in simple armchairs in her office, she with cheese and bread, me with nothing. I pull my legs up under me. Listen like a grown-up to funeral details without starting to cry. She tells me that tradition allows three days at most between death and burial and that the ceremony takes about twenty minutes. Everything is decided in advance; the family doesn't need to do anything. Others come to the house with food and from the time of death the family should wear the same clothes right up until the funeral.

Just before the ceremony, those closest to the deceased are supposed to make a rip in their clothing.

Rain beats against the window and I hear the steady tick of a clock on the wall behind my chair. It feels like I'm sitting with a friend.

When she begins to describe the final bathing I can no longer hold back my tears. The deceased's body is plunged in a holy bath. Male members of the synagogue do this for men and female members do it for women. She does this too. It happens sometimes that she knows the person she bathes, she sees who it is but at the same time she doesn't. She describes how they clean under the dead person's fingernails, how they wrap the body in fresh linen. There are no pockets as we are all equal before God and cannot take anything from this world into the next. I dry my eyes and say that it's beautiful, that they give this gift to the dead.

Her telephone rings. It's the airline and then the family of the person to be buried in Israel call. I slip on my boots. A puddle has accumulated around my umbrella and I try to mop it up with paper towels from the kitchen. She waves at me and mouths that I should just leave it.

The gates outside the synagogue swing shut behind me and I run through puddles and the pouring rain to catch the number two bus at Kungsträdgården. The driver, with a cap and beard, is listening to hip-hop, the wipers thrum on the windscreen and rain lands like pebbles on the roof. I sit on the only free seat, directly behind the driver, stare out the window at people ducking the deluge, am irritated by the obscenities in the hip-hop lyrics. This is what it will be like when Papa passes over to the other side. People will be jumping puddles, running for buses. Normal life will keep on going.

2018

Papa and I are sitting at our favourite café on St Paulsgatan. Today the nice barista is here, the one with short red hair and friendly eyes behind round glasses. Our favourite seats are free, the high bar stools by the window. Papa doesn't have any money on him and you can only pay with cash here. He wants to treat me but when I lend him a five-hundred-kronor note he won't take it. He thinks it's embarrassing to pay with such a big note, asks me to do it instead of him. On the other hand he has no problem keeping the change. It's been going on like this for a couple of years now. He puts me in the line of fire if doing something makes him uncomfortable. If he wants to say no to a concert or an interview he asks me to make the call.

He laughs and pretends to look surprised when I call him out on it. Then he tells me:

'You're right.'

But in the end, he still wants me to walk up to the

counter and pay. I touch on the forbidden thought: *He ducks, protects himself rather than me, his daughter.*

I order a caffeine-free latte with soya milk, a regular coffee and a pain au chocolat that I ask them to cut in two. The man at the counter smiles and doesn't flinch at all over the five-hundred-kronor note.

When we've been served and Papa's taken the change, we stare out at the street and he says that the coffee doesn't taste so good. He often says it when we're here. Still, this is our favourite place. The ambience is pleasant and we always meet someone we know. It's fun sitting by the window looking at all the different characters and dogs that pass.

'Papa . . . I did something very brave.'

'Tell me!'

'I was at the synagogue. To talk about your funeral'.

His eyes open wide:

'Wow! You're so smart, much smarter than I've ever been!'

He wants me to tell him everything, where I went, was it in the synagogue itself or in the offices, what the funeral will cost and what the cheapest option might be:

'How long were you in there?'

He doesn't remember telling me a couple of weeks ago that he has to be buried in the Jewish Cemetery. I laugh:

'I understand that, because you change your mind pretty often. Sometimes you want to be buried in the Jewish Cemetery, sometimes you want to be cremated, even though it goes against your religion.'

He thinks about it a minute, comes to the conclusion that the Jewish Cemetery really is the only proper place. Though maybe he could still be cremated.

When he gets confused he says:

'I want what's cheapest. I want to talk with an expert.'

'Papa, you're the expert here.'

His eyes start to shine. Now he wants to go to the synagogue as well. Can I book an appointment for him? Now, right away? We speak loudly, ignoring the fact that we're sitting in a café. I ask him what he wants to talk to them about.

'I want them to know that I'm a Jewish boy from the Bronx. I want to tell them about my mother.'

I rub his back, move his coffee cup many times to prevent it from being knocked to the floor by his gesticulations. We get looks full of affection from the people working there. I wonder will I ever manage to come here again, the day Papa is no more.

We dip our halves of pain au chocolat in our coffees. When we've been sitting for an hour, talking about life as it passes on the street, death, the approaching inevitable, Papa says that next time we come here he wants me to sit on his right side so that he can hear what I'm saying. He hears much worse in his left ear. We laugh at the fact that he leaves it until now to tell me, when we've already been talking for such a long time and about such important things. Then he wants to go back to the store.

When we cross the road, Papa lifts both his arms and sways. It's like he's trying to remember how to do something.

He tests the air with his arms and splayed fingers. The wind lifts his jacket as he steps gingerly from the curb into the road. He looks at me, wants me to see how well he did it, shouts so that everyone in the street can hear him:

'This is my new way of doing it. It works, I can fly!'

2018

In my breathing space, the place I go when I dance tango, I meet men's hands. I lean my breast against their chest, rest my one arm and a hand across their shoulders. I press tight up against them to feel where they take me. I glide in tango shoes on powdered floors, bare-backed in my black dress from Buenos Aires. Sometimes their hands rest just there, on my bare skin. I like it. I listen to the music and relax, letting someone else decide the steps. For a moment I leave time and space behind.

When I get home late at night Lasse and I talk in the kitchen. We go through what we've been writing. Lasse sips a small glass of whisky. The children sleep. I long for more time to be with him and the family.

2018

Papa has been picked up by the police. It's happened several times now. He can be lost for hours. In the middle of winter. He's been found next to rubbish bins, holding on for dear life. Strangers have taken him into their buildings to get warm. They call my number.

'I'm so terribly sorry,' I'm forced to answer, 'but I really need to ask you to call the police or an ambulance. I'm trying to get my father into a home for the elderly and I need to have examples of all these incidents on the record.' Everyone agrees to phone.

In one week I send the case worker at least five emails. I call, write, nag. Papa needs assisted living NOW. What will it take to convince them that the situation is serious? I write in capital letters but am careful to keep my tone friendly. I report my concern to the social welfare authorities and ask Papa's friends to do the same. I ask to speak to higher-ups. I don't relent. I am a pain in the arse and I'm not ashamed. I write emails at night, in the morning and during the day. I've downloaded an app that lets me record all my phone conversations and I send sound files to the case worker of Papa confused, talking to whoever found him. Kungsholmen District Office is furnished with all the proof I can lay my hands on.

Papa's case worker calls, suggests that she, home services, Papa's friends and I all gather for a meeting. She wants us to discuss 'how we together can alleviate the situation'. I tell her that it's out of the question. My father does not need us to have this sort of conversation. He needs care, *professional care.*

We manage to keep a civil tone, the case worker and myself. I like her and I feel that she likes me. But it's going too slowly and she has all the power.

'One problem is that your father runs a store,' she tells me, 'and therefore home services can only come once a day. Before someone is eligible for placement in a home they need to have tried getting by with visits from home services several times a day. Your father's case is complicated, and unfortunately the decision isn't entirely up to me.'

At night, when the rest of the family are fast asleep, I read reviews and compare different homes for the elderly: Golden Anniversary Home, Jewish Home for the Aged, Malmgården, Riket, Sophiahemmet ... Pictures of velvet sofas with lace doilies, activity calendars, baking and bingo. 'Wednesdays are hotdog days in our lunchroom.' Would he be happy living in a place like that?

Then I see Adagården. A home for the elderly three

hundred metres from Papa's store! The reviews are good, it has a nice courtyard and a pretty roof terrace. In a rush of excitement I attack the keyboard. Sweating. THIS is where Papa should go. If Papa could live here he'd be a stone's throw from Mariatorget, maybe he could hold on to the store, friends could easily come and visit and we could still sit by the fountain and eat ice cream.

2018

A blues concert has been going for an hour and a half already. I thought it would have ended by now, but the young vocalist perched on a chair, eyes closed, still plucks at the strings of his guitar. I sneak in among the dozen people sitting in the audience. They listen, nod in time with the music. Papa sits at the back, drums his thigh with one hand. Despite his confused state he still arranges concerts at least once a week. When I sidle in he jumps to attention and smiles, turns back towards me and whispers:

'This is the best concert ever!'

I can't count the number of times he's said that in the past few years. The singer is far from ready to stop singing or stop telling anecdotes from America's Deep South. Papa points to the man's braces and asks:

'Do you think I would look good in those?'

I tell him that we probably could find a pair for his nine-tieth birthday. I get tired of the music, start flipping through my phone, hide it under my jacket so the performer doesn't see what I'm doing.

An hour later the young musician blows his nose, strums a final chord and tells us at last that he needs to run and catch his bus. Some audience members help clear the chairs and tables. Papa, as per usual, counts the ticket sales directly after the performance. The only difference being that these days he can no longer really count. His friend George sits next to him. Although George has Parkinson's, hands always shaking, he still has his wits about him. They sit there like the two old men they are, their backs turned, counting banknotes. Now and again Papa raises his voice and yells:

'It has to be fair! The musicians always get their half!'

As if George had suggested something else.

In the car on the way home Papa gets angry when I complain that the concert was too long.

'In New York my concerts could go on for hours. Nobody ever complained. If you pay for a ticket you should be happy if you get more than your money's worth.'

I point to the fact that people didn't have TVs and mobile phones back then, maybe that had something to do with it.

'I'll think about it,' he mutters and lets his attention drift out the window.

Seconds later he is certain of the answer.

'The concert could have been longer.'

Home again, sitting in the kitchen with a late-night sandwich, I ask in a roundabout way how he would feel about moving into the Jewish home for the elderly. I'm ranking all the homes, there is a long list of people waiting to get into Adagården and I need some alternatives. For a second I thought that Papa might be able to help me with this difficult decision. The conversation gets too complicated, Papa is unable to take in the information and shouts:

'What do you want from me? I haven't even seen all these places.'

I tell him that the Jewish home has bigger apartments than the other places, that they have a courtyard with a fountain and that they celebrate Shabbat on Fridays; family members are welcome for dinner then:

'They even have a synagogue!'

He says he doesn't care. He wants to live with all kinds of people, not just Jews.

I insist on asking more questions. He gets anxious, wants me to write it all down on paper, draw maps, write down dates. I regret bringing this up; I'm already sure that Adagården would be the best place. He puts his sandwich on the table, has a vague thought, something about this conversation reminds him of other ones we've had recently.

'So what happens to the store?'

I trip over the words, get tangled and scared. Finally I say what has to be said:

'Soon we will probably have to close it.'

He looks me right in the eyes:

'Then I might as well die right away.'

1993

I'm nineteen and taking the train from Stockholm to Paris.
I live there, attending a school for actors. Papa sees me off
at the station but he doesn't wait for the train to leave. He
walks down the platform with a rhythm different from
others. His back tells me that he's sad, that he's older. His
neck is slightly bent.

He has his own apartment now, in Fredhäll; he seems to
both like it and not. He says that none of the neighbours
talk to him, not a single one says hello, 'They're so fucking Swedish!'

The train starts to roll and I turn to look out the window.
Still a bit shaken that he has so little money that he was
going to buy a second-hand shirt at the charity shop. I
should have cut his hair before I left; he won't spend money
on a haircut. And at the station he wanted to buy me lunch,
searched his pockets for some crumpled notes. It was expensive and didn't even taste good.

I've been on my own for a year now. I live in a *chambre
de bonne* directly under a rooftop in Paris and look out on

to Notre-Dame every morning when I wake up. I go to a theatre school with students from every continent, I make new friends, learn to stand on my hands and portray all the elements: water, fire, air and earth. I have my own money and eat cheap Indian food or bread from bakeries. My thoughts are in French, my feet walk across bridges and I kiss beautiful boys. The air in Paris is filled with exhaust fumes and disgusting men hide in the metro waiting to grope you. I call Papa from phone booths and write metre-long letters to friends. I learn all about acting. For the first time I'm going to a school where I feel at home. I'm both free and lonely.

2018

I'm sitting in my cupboard. The one I've been trying to transform into a recording studio. I'm recording an audiobook, making mistakes, not getting enough fresh air, not accustomed to managing all the equipment myself. I'm having trouble concentrating. Outside the cupboard door my mobile phone rings. I forgot to turn it off and stumble out, tripping over my dressing gown. Informal dress is the only advantage to working from home.

'Hello?'

'Hi, I'm calling from social services. We wonder if your father would like to accept a place at Adagården?'

'What? You mean like right now? Right away?'

'That's right. We need your decision within forty-eight hours.'

I've been waiting for this phone call for three long months that have felt like an eternity. Papa has been travelling so much with the taxi service for the elderly that he has used up all his allocation of subsidised rides. This past week has been total chaos. For real. With the lack of taxi service, everything that worked half okay isn't working at all. I say thank you and hastily scratch some information on an old newspaper. Breathless, I phone him:

'I have good news!'

'Tell me!' He laughs and says that I have to wait until he's sitting down.

I tell him that he can move into an apartment in the same street as the store, that we can see it in an hour. As excited as I am, I hear him shout:

'Wow! I can't believe it!'

I bike through slush, slide on icy puddles, cycle on pavements. A woman shouts at me that I should look at the signs. My strong thigh muscles move me faster than cars. Drenched in sweat, I arrive at Papa's store. A bluegrass lesson is taking place and one of Papa's friends is there drinking coffee.

The guests file out, hugging Papa, offering congratulations. Someone takes out the rubbish. I zip up his jacket and hand in hand we walk down the hill. He looks at his watch, wants to time exactly how long it takes to walk to the home. It takes six minutes. He laughs:

'That's way too long!'

I call the woman who's going to show us the room, get Papa to blow his nose. He walks off to toss the tissue away when the woman arrives. She looks tough, has tattoos, greasy hair. Will she be nice to Papa? She doesn't smile but gives Papa's hand a hearty shake.

We walk inside, take the lift up, step through a glass door with a key code and go down a long corridor with blue doors. One of the doors is slightly open and I see a man in a wheelchair, eyes closed, mouth wide open. A woman passes pushing her walking aid. She's nodding all the time. Papa whispers:

'So I'm supposed to live with old people?'

An attendant working on the floor smiles as she passes, stops to joke with Papa. After a moment he laughs and kisses her cheeks, repeats his new mantra:

'I can't believe it.'

We step into the room that might soon be his. It's empty except for an adjustable bed in one corner, a red plastic protective cover stretched over the mattress. We don't look there. We look out the window. At the school across the street. At the trees. Papa rests his hands on the windowsill, sees children running across the school playground and snow hanging off the bare branches. He stands silent for a moment, turns to the woman and me and says:

'This is going to be incredible.'

He doesn't see the worn paint on the walls, doesn't reflect on the fact that someone recently died here. The woman softens, takes photos of things that are shabby, promises the room will be repainted and that she can request an extra storage unit in the cellar as the room is so small.

We meet more staff; they all smile except one who clearly thinks it's the dementia speaking when Papa talks about his concerts. He already wants to arrange music evenings here at the home too. So it's decided. In three days Papa moves in.

2018

Papa's friends help Lasse and I move things into the home. We work for hours, hanging curtains, putting up paintings, screwing together bookcases and filling them with as many books as possible. Papa is waiting in the store. Sometimes he gets someone to help him call me:

'What's going on?' he shouts into the phone.

At five in the evening Papa and I finally walk down the street towards Adagården, arm in arm. At the entrance tears start coursing down his cheeks. Maybe he realizes what is happening, that he's moving into a nursing home. Somewhere, deep inside, I suspect he feels relief. When he steps into his room, sees all his books, paintings and posters, he cries even more.

'Thank you, thank you,' he says in a voice thick with emotion.

One of the attendants has just placed a bouquet of flowers on his desk. She gets red-eyed too, holds up her arm so that we can see the hairs standing on end. She whispers:

'It's so lovely when the family gets the room in order

before the tenants move in.' She presses my hand. 'My name is Lena.'

That evening, under the light of his desk lamp, Papa and I eat in his room. The dining room would be too much of a shock for both of us. Sliced sausage and beans on porcelain painted with blue flowers, and a glass of loganberry juice, sweet and pink. Things we've never eaten or drank in all our lives. I look around and see a resemblance to the apartment in Fredhäll. But this is better, cosier, decorated with love. He eats the last of the potatoes and sauce with his fingers. I don't say anything.

When we've finished we go and inspect the day room. The other residents have all already gone to bed. We watch the communal television for a while but Papa is more interested in the bookshelf out in the hallway. He asks one of the staff if he might buy a book or trade one for one of his own? He takes off his socks and walks barefoot. I wonder if you are allowed to walk barefoot in the hallway here?

Lena seems to understand that it's time for me to go home and that I don't really know how to do it. She asks Papa if he'd like to chat a while and lays a friendly hand on his shoulder.

'I guess I have no choice,' he says in an attempt to joke.

'No, Papa, it's not that way at all,' I tell him and give him a hug.

Lena smiles and assures him that he's still in charge. Papa looks at her, his next question is pure and honest.

'But, what do you want from me?'

'I just want to chat with you for a while.'

Before I go I whisper to Lena that he isn't wearing a nappy. She nods, still softly holding his hands. I take two bags of rubbish left from the move, walk towards the exit. I turn, see Lena's friendly eyes looking into Papa's, and his looking back into hers.

I go. Papa stays. A glass door closes behind me with a click. Papa is locked in now. I glance once more inside and I see them walk together into Papa's room. In the lift I could cry but, surprised, I meet my reflection in the lift mirror. It was such a long time ago since I met my own gaze. There I am, two tired eyes in a face both worn and beautiful.

When I get out on the street I fill my lungs with cold winter air. I dump the rubbish and wrap the scarf an extra time around my neck. Snow falls silently and I walk home. The streets are almost empty. Someone else has the responsibility now.

1996

I live in New York, have started a theatre company here with classmates from the school in Paris. Papa has flown over to see our first production and to meet friends. He manages on his own, knows the city like he knows the back of his hand. He sleeps on a mattress on the floor of the tiny hovel I inhabit in Brooklyn. The radiator hisses and I have practically no furniture. He doesn't complain, is as happy as a child when he gets to hang out with me and nibble biscotti.

Every morning we eat bagels and drink coffee at a diner around the corner. Policemen frequent the place. Italian mixes with the café radio. Everybody shouts. We laugh at the spectacle. If only the coffee wasn't so weak. Papa leafs through the *New York Times* while I memorize my lines.

Evenings, when I'm working at the restaurant, he waits at one of the tables, charms the head waiter and gets a bite to eat from the chef. Long into the night he sits there, waiting for me to finish. After closing I walk exhausted at his side to the subway station. He says that I'm a 'hard-working woman'. It's true, I am. I rehearse early in the morning in the basement of a church and then work until late at night. Sometimes at night I scurry, almost asleep, over endless dark pavements, looking up only when I get to a junction. Daily life in New York City.

On the subway Papa talks about himself and his poems, making up for the hours spent waiting silently in the restaurant. I tune him out, close my eyes, take a break.

A few days later at a former slaughterhouse, now a trendy bar in Williamsburg, we stage our play. The streets here are still untouched by commerce and the buildings are raw. Inside the concrete bunker where we perform there's a pool with fish swimming in illuminated green water. We don't have theatre lights. We point handheld torches to light one another. Like spotlights, they reveal exactly what we wish them to reveal and cast shadows where we want them. Our budget is non-existent and all of our decor is made of junk and leaves gathered during the autumn. It smells like earth. The production is a gem.

Papa comes with two women; they watch the show and then go to sit at the bar. Papa sips a cider. We actors sit with them a while and then go to break down the set. Papa is in his element and I leave him at the bar surrounded by friendly New Yorkers. Everywhere he goes he gets adopted.

It's one o'clock in the morning by the time I'm ready to take a taxi to our side of Brooklyn. The fluorescent ceiling lights burn bright and the audience have all gone home. I can't find Papa. Did he leave with someone without telling me? We ask the owner, who points to a table at the back. There he is, fast asleep without a care in the world. He must have climbed up there to lay down. Two bottles stand next to his head. I know for sure that he didn't drink them. But he's sleeping sweetly, like always, able to fall asleep wherever we are. He could walk through thunder without hardly blinking. Pouring rain runs off him like water off a duck's back, and no matter how red from cold his hands are, he never says he's freezing. If he steps on a nail he won't notice until he sees blood on his sock. It's the same when a pen maliciously leaks in his breast pocket, or if he spills food in his lap; he remains oblivious. But he cares that his hair is combed, that his cheeks are shaved and he has no problem flying across the Atlantic to see his daughter in a play, if he has the money. Now he's sleeping like a baby, hands tucked under his cheek on a bar table in Brooklyn. I wake him; he sits up surprised. The next day he flies home to his life in Sweden, and I continue with my never-ending daily routine.

2012

It doesn't matter where I live, where I work, he'll always come and see me. In Paris, when I'm studying there, he squats on a mattress in my tiny rooftop garret and quickly develops a crush on my theatre teacher. She's from the former Yugoslavia. When I'm in Malmö, in the south of Sweden, hosting a live TV programme for children, he's already sitting in the audience at 7.15. Before that he sat watching me in make-up. Sometimes when I'm working in the smallest of studios he'll squeeze in behind the monitor and take in everything on the screen. Quietly and with great curiosity he sits and admires the film equipment. Proudly I present him to colleagues, making sure he has the best seat in the house. He loves watching me work, but he doesn't always love the productions I'm in. Even when I was a child performing in children's groups he would offer his honest opinion, telling me if he thought it was good or lousy.

Now he's just seen me in a crime drama on TV. As soon as the credits start running he calls me to say:

'That was the worst shit I've ever seen!'

I'm with my in-laws when the call comes. Sitting among porcelain figurines in a suburb where all the houses look the same. His review stings and I tell him he's insensitive. Fortunately no one in Lasse's family hears me when I shout or when I cry. A few minutes later I call him back. I shout so I'm spraying saliva. That role was one of the most painful roles I've ever played. He probably didn't mean me. Just the programme. Crime dramas aren't his thing. But he can't differentiate. He says he's sorry and we stay friends. I can never be angry with him for longer than a moment. Is he ever angry with me?

We hang up. Lasse is putting Nikolai to bed and I go out for a walk in the falling light. Through windows I see televisions lighting up living rooms and I smell lilacs. I'm thinking that I never said anything about him not being so great in that tiny role he had in *The Girl Who Played with Fire*. He played an irritated man in a synagogue, was hired as an extra but threw in a line spontaneously and the director chose to keep it. I wouldn't dream of saying something that nasty, like saying that he overacted.

2018

They call from the home and are wondering where Papa is. They know that he was hosting a concert and were expecting him to be late, but it's almost eleven now. On most days the staff walk him to the store in the morning and walk back with him in the afternoon. He complains that they get him at half-past four, which he thinks is way too early. He believes he makes his money between five and six; that's when people pass by on their way home from work. Until now the staff have always been able to convince him to leave with them.

I call George who was supposed to walk Papa home after tonight's concert. Music and loud voices fill the background when he answers. He doesn't say hello, just shouts:

'We're in a bar drinking Bloody Marys!'

He promises to bring Papa to the home soon. I hear Papa shout:

'Hey, I want to talk to my daughter too!'

We manage to exchange a few words before I say good-night and hang up. Tonight he'll go to bed later than I will. I wonder what the staff at the home think.

2018

Papa has a high fever and a terrible cough. A nurse from Adagården phones. It's been a few months now and I've finally learned the names of most of the staff. She says they're going to have to prescribe antibiotics. I say okay, but I'm worried he might have an allergic reaction; I don't recall him ever having taken antibiotics before.

A few days later he's back on his feet. I want him to get out of the home and spend some time in the store. He hasn't been there for ten days. I march into his room and call out:

'Hey, Papa!'

'Hey, Papa!' he answers like an echo.

Hugs and kisses.

'I thought we might hang out in the store today,' I tell him, buttoning one of his shirt buttons.

'What store?'

'Your store.'

'I have a store?'

'Yeah, you know . . . just down the street.'

He looks at me, confused. I pick up my phone:

'Do you want to see pictures?'

'Sure!'

I google 'Folklore Centrum', immediately get loads of results, hold the phone in front of him, zoom into the pictures so that he can see better. He points at a picture of himself standing in front of the store's bookshelves:

'Is that my store?'

'Yeah, you've had it for over forty years.'

'Wow, it's beautiful.'

He steps out into the hallway. Wants to go there right away. His memory is back. I exhale, at the same time I feel tension in my chest and arms.

In the lift he stares at me as if his eyes are turned inwards. It's the gaze of a person with dementia. I remind him where we're going:

'We're going to the store.'

At the same time as I say it I'm thinking that maybe we should go back up again. This was a bad idea.

'Or maybe we'll just have coffee on the terrace instead? It's nice up there . . .'

'No, I want to go to my store.'

Oh well, whatever happens will happen. Either he'll survive or he'll die. We step outside and as soon as the sunlight falls on his head he's greeted by someone on the street:

'Hi, Izzy! Still going strong?'

'Yep,' Papa answers.

He knows where he is, points down the street showing precisely in which direction the store lies. A few metres from the door there's a shout from the restaurant across the street.

'Izzy, come in and have a coffee!'

We sit at an outside table, are served two lattes with barista hearts drawn in the froth. It's on the house. The owners have been our heroes every day for the past year or so, walking across the street to bring Papa his lunch. If he wasn't in the store they'd call me. I will for ever be thankful to them. I look at the clock. This is taking more time than I had imagined.

After a while I go inside the restaurant and ask if they can make sure that Papa gets into the store.

'I need to leave now ... but he would love to sit in the sun a while longer.'

'Of course,' they say, and I hurry with uneasy steps towards my meeting as planned. I wasn't prepared for this. That he would have forgotten the store.

2018

I'm packing and packing when all I really want to do is spend time with Papa. There are thousands of books, magazines and newspaper clippings that need to be sorted before I close up the store. Several of Papa's friends have been helping me, but today I'm by myself. It's an unusually warm summer. And although I've placed three desk fans strategically, whirring and turning, the sweat is running down my back. I blow dust from book pages and fill rubbish bag after rubbish bag with stuff that can be thrown out. Even though the place is such a mess and feels sad, I love being here. It's easier I think to pack up the place now, while Papa is still alive and just a couple of hundred metres down the same street. He hardly ever mentions the store anymore. If I take him out for a walk to Mariatorget, I make sure that we take alternate routes to avoid him recognizing the street he knew so well.

People have been asking about buying the lease. They've sent emails or slipped handwritten notes through the letter box in the door. They don't understand that Papa has only

been subletting the place all these years. They barge in without knocking. I don't mind some questions, but others feel
like greedy fingers trying to grab what was always Papa's.
I start locking the door. Papa always left it open. Maybe it
would be better to pack at night; I'm so visible through the
storefront windows. On the other hand I get a lot of friendly
waves. Neighbours, the postman, the building's caretaker,
all asking me how things are going.

A man knocks on the door, just as sweaty as I am, stares
curiously at all the boxes of books piled high. He asks how
things are with my dad, how old he is now and if he has
any other family. I answer politely, even though I don't have
the time. He claims that he and Papa are old friends, but I
can't remember ever having seen him. He looks down into
one of the rubbish bags:

'The thing is,' he says, 'I write obituaries for one of the
major newspapers.'

I turn my back and answer curtly:

'Excuse me, I need to get back to work.'

'Of course,' he says.

Still he's there pushing his business card at me.

'Just call me if anything happens.'

The minute the door closes I pick up my phone and call
one of Papa's closest friends, a writer and journalist.

'I want you, nobody else but you, to write Papa's
obituary!'

He promises.

Before I've taken a step towards the door to lock it an

older woman walks inside. She asks if she might buy one of the paintings in the window.

'I love the way the light filters through it . . .'

The painting is faded from sunshine and stained with coffee; there isn't even any glass in the frame. I know that it's been hanging on the wall since I was little, but I always thought the image was hard to identify. It's a sketch in watercolours, simple lines, probably depicting a woman at a sewing machine. I hesitate, but think that Papa's walls in the home are covered with paintings and soon enough I'll have more than I could possibly have room for.

'Okay . . .' I say and she eagerly hands me two hundred kronor and hurries off down the street.

Minutes later, after a quick search on the internet, I understand that she stuffed a painting by Bror Hjorth into her bag. I sold it for a fraction of what it was worth.

I sit on the stairs to the cellar. Wipe a dirty hand over my brow and let the gurgling sound of the sewage pipes and the heavy dark of the basement comfort me. Papa isn't dead yet and already the vultures are circling. I rest my head against the metal banister that once was white but is now sticky black. It feels good as it cools my forehead.

In a couple of hours, a man from an antiquarian bookstore is coming to value Papa's library. He arrives at the exact appointed time, an immaculate briefcase in his hand. Despite the heat he wears a suit jacket and doesn't seem in the least bit sweaty. He runs a finger over Papa's bookshelves.

'Reference books, reference books,' he states with

certainty and decides that he doesn't even want to make a valuation. Instead he questions me about the sale we made to an antiquarian a few years ago. Assures me that we would have been better off selling to him. Leaving, he tells me:

'You should have a garage sale. It'll be fun, people will fight over some of these books. You can charge two hundred kronor per book the first hour, one hundred the second hour and fifty kronor the third. Whatever is left you can let people take for free. You could arrange some live music and sell coffee too. Then it would be an event!'

I should do what Papa does. Shout 'fuck you' to everyone who walks into the store:

'FUCK YOU! FUCK YOU! FUCK YOU!'

I lock the door and in the sticky heat walk down the hill to Adagården. I punch in the key code and though I'm drenched with sweat, run up the four flights of stairs. I'm hit with the place's constant smell of boiled potatoes. As soon as I walk inside, anxiety hits me like an electric shock. I never know how it's going to be when I see him, or if I'll walk into some kind of frightening situation in the hallway. There's a resident, an Estonian, who used to be a prize fighter who can be quite scary. He doesn't speak a word of Swedish. But usually things are calm. I suppose by running up the stairs I'm trying to release some tension. I'm breathless by the time I get to the fourth floor.

Papa sits on the bed and on the desk I spy a tray with napkins, four small coffee cups and a bowl of sugar. He must have had visitors. The ones who love him continue to visit regularly, just like they used to visit him at the store. They come with a guitar on their backs or an instrument tucked under their arms. The sounds of singing, strumming, flute or accordion flow almost daily from his room into the otherwise sleepy corridor. Poetry is read out loud and the accents of foreign visitors loudly fill the day room. The other day Papa shed tears of gratitude over all the visits he receives. He said in a tiny voice:

'I feel so loved.'

I sit next to him on the bed. He is barefoot, feet resting on the floor. Thick toenails. Dry heels.

'What have you been doing today?' he asks.

'Working . . . recording audiobooks and stuff . . .'

I look down at the floor. He nods, calls me a 'hard-working girl' and pulls me close to him. I feel like a liar, packing up the store without asking permission, without him even knowing I'm doing it. He kisses my forehead and in just that moment it feels like he'll live for ever. His fists are still stronger than mine. But I've seen the way he trembles and how he loses his balance if he needs to walk more than thirty metres. Last week he thought that a jug of custard was a glass of water. Sometimes he whistles instead of speaking. It happens that he wants to call his brother Oscar. I don't tell him that Oscar died a few years ago and that almost every stitch of clothing Papa has was left to him by Oscar. Everything fits like a glove; it's just the style that's different.

He forgets a lot. Am I next? How many days, hours,

seconds are left until even I am erased? Does he need to forget me in order to let go?

I tell him that I'll be going away soon:

'I'll be gone for a week.'

'Oh,' he says and sighs. 'I'll miss you, but I'll survive.'

Before I leave to continue packing up the store I take the tray with the coffee cups out to the kitchen. I slot a sizable donation into the coffee tin, the coins rattling as they hit the bottom. Lena, standing at the cooker making dinner, says:

'Sweetie, you really don't need to do that.'

'Oh, yes I do!' I say laughing. 'Papa gets busloads of visitors.'

She smiles:

'I know, it's beautiful. The other day one of his friends started playing guitar here in the dining room. It was so lovely I get goose bumps thinking about it. It made all the residents so happy.'

I want to go over and give her a hug, but we don't know each other well enough yet, so I say:

'Thanks, you and all the others working here are the best in the whole world.'

2018

Natasha and I are playing on the beach. We're on a little island in Greece, searching for flat stones that turn into fairy tales. We've been playing the same game for several days. One evening, after the heat settles, we splash ankle-deep in a lagoon. The water is turquoise and warm after a day in the sun. I find a big stone and sit down on a large rock. Natasha sits close, waiting eagerly for the story I'm about to begin.

'Once upon a time there was a grandpa who time after time outwitted death. He was compelled to do it, so great was his desire to eat ice cream with his two beloved grandchildren.'

She's all ears. Laughing and splashing her toes in the salty Mediterranean. The tale reaches its end and the grandpa turns into a fish.

'Because that way he can still play and swim around his grandchildren's feet.'

Natasha, serious now, stares out over the blue water and with the certainty of a five-year-old says:

'Mama. The sea goes on for ever. I think Grandpa is dead now.'

She looks right at me.

'For real. I think he is.'

I answer that I don't think so, that I just talked to him a couple of days ago. She insists:

'No, Mama, Grandpa is dead now.'

'Natasha, you'll have me crying if you say that.'

'But you don't need to. Grandpa is a fish in the sea and can play with our feet. And look here!'

She lifts her hand and shows me a large pink stone:

'Here's Grandpa's heart.'

The minute we get back to the hotel I grab the phone and call Papa.

2018

Every time I visit the home I bring one of the paintings from the store. It's almost all packed up now, all the books have been photographed, catalogued and carefully packed in boxes. I want Papa's collection to end up in a good place. There is some serious interest from the United States. The poetry I've decided to keep myself. I tramp through wet leaves and puddles crusted with ice. Carry painting after painting under my arm. It makes Papa happy. He's stopped pulling them off the walls at night, the way he did in the beginning, when he thought he was in jail.

There's hardly any space on the walls for more art, but when I hammer in a nail for another painting he follows every move I make. Occasionally he'll tell visitors that he lives here now, but when we're eating in the dining room he often thinks that we're at a restaurant. Stressed, he'll start searching through his pockets for money to pay the bill, a movement I recognize from when I was little. So often his eyes opened wide in a sudden panic, he gasped for breath, one hand searching his pockets for the money he might have dropped, the other hand pressed hard against his heart. I soon learned to search as quickly as he could. It was almost always me who found what he was looking for.

Just as I'm about to put a CD into his portable stereo I get a text. It's from the Orthodox rabbi, a man with a long beard, corkscrew sideburns and a hat. He would often stop by the store and visit Papa on holy days, or when they were short of the number of men needed to read the prayers. Papa would always lock the store and follow the rabbi to the synagogue. He'd talk about it for days afterwards, feeling chosen, saying that his mother would have been proud. The message from the rabbi reads, 'It's Hanukkah, could my sons come and visit Izzy?'

Soon three teenage boys and a boy about seven years old, all in white shirts and black hats, stand in the middle of the room. Papa laughs when they put a kippa on his head and hand him a plate of doughnuts. They light eight coloured candles in a menorah and start singing a Jewish song, so madly loud that the whole floor must be able to hear it. They are absolutely sober, but they still sound like a gang of drunken sailors.

Papa is sobbing, removes his glasses and says: 'I can't believe it! I just can't believe it!' Then he starts singing too, following the others as best he can. The room fills with warmth and energy. The candles flicker.

2018

I see him coming. The man who owns the lease. I'm tense. Try to hold myself together. Just need to hand him a bunch of keys, go out and lock the door behind me for the very last time. The store, naked as a newborn infant, will be given to someone else. I smile and say hi. He asks how it is with Papa.

'Well, it's all right.'

I show the light in the cellar that doesn't always work, the toilet seat that's coming off its hinges, the tap that leaks. I hand him the keys, still in control of my emotions. We go out and he locks the door. I show him how it works, how to jiggle the key in the lock. I give the door handle a last caress and say a brisk:

'Goodbye, store!'

We walk in opposite directions. I pretend I have to rush off to work but slip around the corner and wait. I go back when I'm certain he's left the neighbourhood, sit down in one of the doorways across the street and look at my childhood home. The door and the window frames a shiny green. All that remains are twenty or so stickers on the front door from different music festivals that I was too tired to scrape away.

Soon a florist is moving in here. At least it's something beautiful.

2019

'So when will I get to see you?'
'Soon, Papa. I'll come by this weekend.'

He always asks me that just before we hang up the phone.
That, and how the family is doing. He's been living at
Adagården for six months now. Christmas came and went,
and I closed the store. We exchange a few words on the
phone during my breaks from rehearsals at the Royal
Dramatic Theatre. I'm replacing another actress in the
performance that in a few weeks will go on a mini-tour
to France. Sometimes I hurry to him before picking up
Natasha at pre-school. When I walk into his room he's often
at his desk, tearing paper, photographs, money, napkins,
into tiny, tiny strips and pieces.

Early one morning, a few days before the tour, I see that
I've missed several phone calls during the night. My hands
sweat. I press the phone hard against my ear. The message
box tells me that the first call came at half-past three in
the morning. A tense voice says, 'Hi, I'm a staff nurse at

Adagården. We suspect that your father might have had a stroke. Please call us as soon as you get this message.' Then two more phone calls from the same number.

I squat down, use the floor for support, call Papa's ward:

'Do you need me to come at once?'

'No, better let him rest,' a friendly woman's voice says on the other end, 'he's just back from the hospital emergency ward.'

She describes how angry Papa was when the ambulance came. It took four people to hold him down; they had to sedate him before they could get him into the ambulance.

I make it to the theatre, manage to run through my lines, do some voice warm-ups. Then I run to Stureplan, grab the first metro train, hurry into a bakery, sprint up the stairs and into Papa's room without saying hello to anyone in the hallway.

He's asleep. Jerks a tiny bit when I come into the room. I sit down at his bedside with my winter jacket still on. His eyes are closed but he starts jabbering as soon as he wakes up. I feed him a piece of vanilla bun. It's buttery and crisp. The whole room fills with the scent of freshly baked cake as soon as I open the bag. He says something inaudible and smiles. Even though I can't see him do it, I know that the hand he can now hardly move is making the sign for 'perfect'. The cake tastes perfect. After three tiny bites he doesn't want more.

2019

He lies on the bed in a nappy and a T-shirt. Enraged, he has in some inexplicable manner been able to kick his blanket off, despite his body no longer obeying him. The staff have left him alone to calm down. When I come into the room his eyes light up. I lower the rails around the bed, kick off my shoes and make room for myself next to him. His hand, slow from the stroke, searches in the air, trying to embrace me. I help him and he sighs deeply when he finally has his arms around me.

After a while I start to get restless. I get up from the bed, take out the fresh bread I purchased for the day. A Danish breakfast loaf with poppy seeds, like the ones that we used to buy at Gunnarsson's bakery when I was little and it was my birthday. Luxury bread. I ask if he wants a piece. He nods and I place a tiny crumb on his tongue. He closes his mouth in slow motion, hiccups, falls asleep, his mouth open. Afraid he might choke, I fish the bread out. I sit beside him and compose a text message to his friends explaining the situation. It's already dusk. Will he die now?

I lay down beside him again, rest my ear against his chest. It doesn't move. Has he stopped breathing? Should I call for help or just let him die in peace and quiet without the staff running in? Maybe I should just let him peacefully slip away in the warmth of my arms.

He coughs and gains his breath again. A big cry pours out from me. Even though he's asleep he seems to still sense that something is wrong. He hugs me clumsily, with eyes still closed he asks me something that is incomprehensible. As if he's talking in his sleep. I know he is asking me why I'm crying.

'Because I'm afraid you're going to die and because I love you so much,' I sob.

With eyes half closed, and against the effects of the stroke, he gathers strength. He shouts to the ceiling:

'But I'm still here!'

A handful of words and an invisible fist punching the air.

'Yes, you're right about that . . .'

He smiles, satisfied when he hears me laugh.

We lie still a while. Through the window I can hear someone throwing bottles in the recycling bin down the street. Papa falls asleep. His skin is so soft these days, the staff put on his lotion with extra care.

2019

I've had a cold, haven't dared visit for fear of infecting Papa. Today I feel better and visit with Natasha. We buy three *semlor*, the traditional cream cakes served during Lent. We watch as they're carefully placed in a box and tied with ribbons with the name 'Konditori Chic' printed on them. Natasha proudly carries the package so that the cakes won't get crushed.

In the dining room Papa sits in a wheelchair, his white T-shirt has a huge coffee stain. He doesn't know that he had a stroke, that he's unable to walk, that it's difficult for us to understand what he's saying. When I try to explain he wants to stand up right away, show me how strong his legs are. He can't.

But he knows who we are. And he recognizes cakes.

We eat them in silence. He manages without help to lift the cake from the plate to his mouth. In three large bites he devours the cardamom, cream and marzipan, while winking at me and Natasha. The staff hover in the background, help me with the wheelchair. We all notice the return of his appetite.

Natasha plays games on her iPad. Today it's okay. She can play while Papa and I look out the dining-room window. I sit tight beside him. We look down on naked trees, at the school opposite:

'Imagine how beautiful this will be in the spring,' I say. 'Then we go out to the park and watch the fountain.'

2019

I'm in France. I will soon stand on a stage again, in the
bright glare of spotlights. Unreal. As if everything was
make-believe. As if suddenly I'll be de-masked, exposed as
a fake, or I'll lose my voice. I imagine that I'll hurt my back,
that my father will die, that I'll be forced to fly home, dis-
appointing the director and the whole cast. That something
will happen that will tear me from this dream. But my voice
still holds, my back too, and Papa is alive.

In one scene I'm playing an ageing Casanova, so weak
he can hardly stand, but still wanting to seduce. When we
rehearse I stand with legs splayed, put on a dark voice, play
the 'horny gentleman'. After the run-through the director
says that she wants me to take the scene more seriously:

'I want you to portray a man at the very end of his days.
He longs to, for the very last time in his life, get really close
to a woman. I want it played truthfully, without a trace
of irony.'

In the performance tonight I become Papa. I sit on the
stage in an armchair longing for life, trying to light a fire in

my loins, stumbling towards the front of the stage, pulling myself upright and swirling a white cloth that flies around me. I tap-dance, showing myself and the actress playing opposite that I still have power in my legs. The Casanova I play booms his favourite line out across the stalls:

'BUT ... with my extraordinary seven-mile strides I'll catch you!'

The actress gallops in a wide circle around the stage. Teases, lifts her skirts. I step after her, the fabric flying behind me, feeling pleasure though something is clawing in my chest. It's as if part of me and part of Papa are taking those massive strides.

I catch my breath in an armchair, groaning with desire when the actress climbs up and straddles my thighs. I hold her hips and caress her. She grabs my head and smothers me with her breasts. The Casanova gets what he needs.

2019

I sleep in a hotel room with thick curtains that cover the windows. I've almost forgotten Papa. I trust that the people who've said that they will look after him are doing so. The evening after our second performance I get a text message from Mama: 'All is fine with Izzy. Great mood. We read poetry. He's very clear about what books he wants me to take down off the shelf.'

2019

A deep snow covers the Royal Dramatic Theatre and the bust of August Strindberg outside it. A taxi just drove us from the airport into town. The theatre company's shoes and luggage sink deep into the fresh, clean white. We hug farewell, thanking each other for fantastic performances and a wonderful trip. I walk into the theatre to empty my dressing room and leave my key card. My work here is over. It feels okay. Strangely enough it feels like theatre is a closed chapter for me. Standing on the stage doesn't feel important anymore.

I take the bus home, snow melting to puddles around my shoes, the window cool against my forehead. I'm content, played my role well, remembered my lines even though I've been wondering if my brain would burst from all the strain of these last years. I bought presents for Lasse and the kids. I look forward to some rest, time for my family. I want to write, and I want to clean. My desk at home is a mountain of chaos, untouched for months.

2019

I awake the following morning, raise the blinds to a snow-white Stockholm. After kissing my family good morning I call the home. Dialling the number feels almost unfamiliar. A nurse answers and I ask:

'How are things with Papa?'

'Uhm . . .'

She hesitates.

'He's only been awake a short time and he refuses to eat. It started yesterday evening.'

I trip over my unpacked suitcases, pat the children on the cheek, apologize to Lasse and throw myself out into the cold. The breath wells out from my mouth. I try the bike but my tyres get stuck in the snowdrifts. I take the car out. Find a place to park from where I won't have to move it for several days.

When I open the door to his room he's sitting right across from me in the wheelchair. His head is tilted back and his face is birdlike thin. I hardly recognize him.

I caress his cheek, even though I feel scared by it:

'Papa, I'm here now ...'

He doesn't wake up. Not even when I raise my voice. Not even when I squeeze his arm hard.

A nurse enters:

'Perhaps it's best if we speak privately?'

I know what those words mean. Papa would have known what 'privately' means. He would have looked at me, made a silly face and rolled his eyes in complicity if he heard those words.

Inside the office she talks as if we are discussing the weather, doesn't even bother to close the door:

'Well, Israel hasn't eaten anything since yesterday evening, and he's hardly been awake since yesterday afternoon. Because of that we'll only give him palliative care. This means that we'll no longer try to make him eat or drink.'

When I walk out into the corridor I let my hair hide my face. I feel shame, though I know I shouldn't. I don't want anyone to see me. I am the loser; soon everyone will see me go to pieces.

Inside the room he's still asleep, his bird face hanging loose against his shoulder. Staff members come in and with a harness on a lift they move him from the wheelchair to the bed. For a moment Papa floats in the air.

2019

The streetlights sway and in their beams the snow falls in furious drifts. The street below Papa's window is white. The school playground is white. And Papa is dying. This time for real. It's almost four in the morning and he hasn't opened his eyes since yesterday afternoon. He's tired. So tired. Sleeps deeply. Mouth open. Hacks sometimes, is silent again. There are periods in which his breathing is heavy. I hold his hand. Kiss his brow. Mama was on her way to the mountains but turned back when she saw my text message: 'Papa is dying now.' She walked into the room with skis tucked under her arm, placed them against one of the cupboards and let me hang my arms around her neck like a little child. Now she lies on a mattress in the little kitchen, sometimes her snoring keeps time with Papa's breathing. But she's been awake almost the whole night.

I can't sleep, just want to cry when I close my eyes. I jump as soon as he makes a sound. Sometimes I lay down for a minute or so on a mattress in the bathroom. It's the only place I can, for a few short moments, rest.

2019

'Mmm ... there, there ... my best papa, the best papa in the world, best, best papa ...'

I repeat the mantra. He seems calmer when I caress his forehead, whisper, pat. It's so clear, the calming effect of touch. He pants. His breathing stops. He starts panting again. I wet his lips, his tongue. Tell him that I love him. We start again, over and over. His hand and his skin are still his.

I'm most frightened when I'm not there beside him, when I need to run out and buy something, need something from the dining room, need to let someone in from the entrance downstairs. Some people don't understand that every second counts now. As soon as I leave the room my heart is under attack, my chest, my lungs. I have a hard time breathing and need to get back immediately. When I'm physically close to him I'm only loving and exhausted. It happens that I'll pick up my phone and flip through Facebook. Even during the very short intervals when he's awake. Am I horrible?

There were eight of us here with him today. Tomorrow two others say they're coming. He is loved, my papa.

2019

I'm here, here, here. I lie down next to him, crowd in, tight beside him on the bed. The thought passes that I'll soon need to empty this last room too. I can't empty any more; I don't have the energy to do it. Strangely enough I'm hungry, eat loads. Maybe I'm making up for my lack of sleep.

Now I wet his gums with a cotton swab. I caress his arm. Does it hurt him if I caress his arm in the wrong direction, against the hairs?

2019

One of Papa's friends, Allen, is in the room singing ragtime blues. He sits bent over his guitar. The sun climbs through the window and warms Papa's blanket. Lasse and Nikolai are also here. I sit next to Papa and hold his hand. When I notice his eyes flutter and then open, I startle, lean in close so he can see me:

'Hi, Papa. Are you awake now?'

He gives me a wide, toothless smile. Smacks his lips like a fish underwater. His cheeks move in and out. Eyes sparkle and he tries to lift his head off the pillow. I can't stop myself from laughing. It's so clear that he wants to kiss me. I lean my cheek against his lips and he kisses me several times with a smacking sound. Like a newborn child he looks around the room and at us, listens to Allen playing.

A few minutes later I rush to the dining room and tell the staff:

'Papa is awake! He says he's hungry. Would it be okay if he had something to eat?'

One of my favourite attendants on the ward says he'll

ask the doctor. Five minutes later he comes into the room holding a tray with vanilla ice cream in small, delicate bowls. The room is filled with guitar and song and the staff feed Papa with a silver spoon. Cold ice cream melts in our mouths. Before, we couldn't understand a word of what he said. Now, when I ask him if he wants more, he yells:

'Yeah!'

And a little while later:

'More!'

Allen sings, 'Candy man, candy man, been here and gone'. We laugh and I'm so happy Nikolai is with us to share this moment. His prince-like curls that I've always adored glisten in the honey-yellow light. Papa's victory roar makes him giggle. This isn't scary. Even Natasha could have been here now. Papa squeezes me while ice cream is spooned into his mouth. One foot beats time against the bed frame and Allen shouts:

'You see! Live music brings you back to life!'

I can see how the emotion seizes Lasse. It's seldom that I've seen tears in his eyes.

2019

Papa's breathing hard. I caress his arm. Since the ice cream yesterday he hasn't had any food or water, wasn't even able to suck the cotton swab I put on his tongue.

They've just rubbed him with moisturizer. They are so considerate in their care. Mama and I turn him so that he doesn't get bedsores.

'Best, best papa ...' I whisper while she piles pillows around his feet. The sheet shouldn't lie heavy on his toes. He breathes easier in this new position. He can't even turn his head now. Ten days ago I helped him with exercises. I moved his legs up and down so that he would one day be able to walk again. My dear, dear papa.

He stops breathing.

I think he's dying now.

2019

He breathes quickly, panting like a dog. One of my best friends, my mother and I are sitting at his bedside. We've lit candles. A nurse I haven't met before is also in the room. Her stiff manner doesn't fit in and she only addresses my mother when she has something to say. The nurse says that Papa is in pain, that she's going to give him medication. I didn't notice that he was feeling any pain. Have I been missing something? Have we let him suffer? My friend, who also is a nurse, whispers:

'No, I didn't notice him having any pain either. But it won't hurt to give him something. Don't let this upset you now.'

The nurse turns to my mother:

'Could you all please leave the room? The night staff and I are going to change Israel and give him a sedative.'

I hesitate but stand, put a hand on his shoulder and say:

'Papa, we'll just be in the dining room. The people here will take care of you. We'll be right back.'

I think I see him nod.

We walk out into the hallway and towards the kitchen. The whole ward is silent, everyone else has already gone to bed. Somehow it feels good, leaving the room and taking a break, seeing something different, making tea. At the same time I'm trying to understand why I'm always supposed to go out when they turn him or change his nappy. How many times have I washed my father, seen him naked? I also puff up the pillows and blankets around his body. Why is his care considered too intimate all of a sudden? Why should a nurse, one that neither Papa nor myself have ever seen before, step in at this stage to do the most private things? I didn't ask for this. Nobody has asked me what I want, or what Papa might want. Who or what are they trying to protect? Papa's integrity? Their own work environment? Or do they do this simply to give the family a chance to rest?

We drink Earl Grey and cherry tea. In the dementia ward there are never any real candles; all the candles on the tables are electric, left there since Christmas. I appreciate their attempts to make the place cosy. I feel a hard pull in my stomach: *Papa's lying in the room, without me.* I pour more hot water into the cups and say:

'This is what symbiosis is like. It was the same when my kids were babies, I knew exactly when they'd wake or when they were hungry. Now I just want to run back to Papa.'

My friend pats me on the cheek. The assistant nurse comes in, stands by the door and whispers:

'You can go in again if you like, we're finished.'

I like him, his Finland Swedish accent is soft, his eyes

friendly and he was one of the first ones here I got to know. I think: *No, don't rush back inside like someone possessed, sit here a moment and catch your breath.* We talk about one thing or another, drag a bed from the store cupboard so that I can place it next to Papa's. The beds will be the same height then; I can rest and still hold his hand. I push the bed in front of me down the hall. It's the middle of the night. I'm tired now. My legs are heavy. Soon it will be three days without rest.

In Papa's room the candles are flickering; we forgot to blow them out. It looks soft, almost cosy. The warmth is mirrored in the glass in all the paintings. I leave the bed and step inside. I stiffen immediately when I see his eyes. They're staring.

'But ... he's dead!'

I turn and see the shocked look on the assistant nurse's face behind Mama's. He blurts out:

'What? He was alive just minutes ago!'

He hurries out into the hallway. A click and clack of wooden clogs.

I bend forward, shut Papa's eyelids as I know one should do. They are still warm, soft; they agree to stay closed. Mama puts her arms around me, as if she wants to lift me or keep me steady so I don't fall over.

'I need space,' I say, and pull free from her arms, thinking at the same time that I might have hurt her feelings.

My friend holds two fingers across Papa's wrist, says that at first she thought she could feel a faint pulse, but now it's gone. I throw a window open, fresh winter air, but no soul flies up to heaven. For me, he is still here, in this room.

I caress his forehead. My friend asks if I want her and Mama to go out. I ask them to stay:

'What I really want to do is kiss his stomach ... but I feel shy.'

'You should do exactly as you feel.'

She says it with a certainty that makes me daring. I carefully lift his T-shirt and his warm belly meets my lips. I lay a cheek on his stomach. There is no breath anymore to make it move.

'I want to lay down beside him.'

'Then you should.'

I lie down behind him. Spoon. Push myself as close as possible, hold his body in my arms. He warms me still. I can still hold him. My friend pulls the bed rail up behind me, so I won't fall out. She lays a shawl over my shoulders. Like in a cradle I lie behind Papa and weep silently, my mother and my friend like a safe shield around us, keeping us safe.

His body cools. Soon it will be uncomfortable. I don't want to be lying beside him when he's cold. That thought makes it natural for me to raise myself, and let go.

Together we straighten his arms and legs. Tuck him inside the sheets of the bed. Lay the blanket neatly on top. He's begun to stiffen. The nurse enters with a plastic wristband in her hand. The type that goes on a newborn. She also checks his pulse:

'I'm sorry for your loss.'

It sounds like she's been trained to say it.

My father's time and date of death has been typed on to the wristband. Did she already prepare it earlier that evening? I refuse to let her put it on Papa's wrist; instead I lay it on the desk. I won't let him be tagged like an object. As soon as she leaves the room I'm tossing it.

Finally she leaves.

Among lighted candles we stay with Papa, eat jelly heart sweets, take turns reading his favourite poem out loud. 'Father Death Blues', by Allen Ginsberg. It's always hung in a frame on the wall in the store, signed twice by Ginsberg himself to make it perhaps even more valuable. On the back, Papa meticulously ordained that I and nobody else should inherit this artwork the day he passes on. We read the poem, over and over.

> Hey Father Death, I'm flying home
> Hey poor man, you're all alone
> Hey old daddy, I know where I'm going
>
> Father Death, Don't cry any more
> Mama's there, underneath the floor
> Brother Death, please mind the store

For me, he's still with us. Somewhere in the room. He always liked 'to hang around'.

*

Year after year, you carried me. High. Sometimes I slept up there. Straddling your shoulders. Bouncing. My tiny hands and arms cupping your cheeks, your newly shaven chin. I rested my head against your warm, balding scalp. We walked home, from pre-school, concerts, dances. Through Stockholm and other towns and cities. Over bridges. In daylight, sun, wind and rain. Winter, morning and evening. Sometimes late at night. I kept lookout, sang, dozed. Slept soundly high up where no one could reach me. Sometimes I sat there for hours. Your hands firmly holding my calves so I would never fall. You sang:

I have a little daughter, her name is Philomène. She's only five years old, but she is my best friend. She knows how to run, how to dance, how to jump. She knows how to do eeeeverything!

And on every walk we took, you'd invent something new your daughter could do. She who is me.

Thank You

This is my story, how I remember it. Some dates and details have been changed and some situations joined in time. My favourite uncle Oscar died earlier than I suggest in this story. Sometimes there were more of us present than indicated. Certain people and places have been given fictional names.

Above all it is you, Papa's friends, who have not been given the space in this story that you deserve. That's because there are simply so many of you and this book would have had too large a cast of characters.

I especially thank those of you who stayed close by my side and gave support to me and Papa these last years: Allen, Buffalo, Danny, George, Göran, Hanna, Markus, Maria, Nalle, Noah, Peter, Ted, Terry and last but not least, the café and sandwich bar En Halv Trappa Ner.

Thank you everyone who invited Papa and I for lunch or dinner when I was a child. Thank you everyone who helped Papa stay in business, the neighbours and people on the street who cared about him, the musicians and artists who played for him, read poetry for him and everyone who helped me tie things up when I closed the store.

A huge thanks also to my beloved husband Lars Demian, who has read every line in this book repeatedly and listened to me go on about it day and night. I'm so grateful that you are in this world with me.

Thank you Mama, Catherine Grandin, for giving me life. Thank you for choosing Izzy to be my father and for choosing Sweden, the both of you together. Thanks for all the books you read to me when I was little and for watching by my side during those last long days.

Thanks Källa and Shari for standing by me when I was going through the worst. Thank you Liv and Åsa who always answer the phone.

Thank you everyone in healthcare who helped Papa this last year. My deepest heartfelt thanks to Ghazwan and Lena. I am touched just by thinking about you.

Anna Nachman, thanks for your friendliness and all your help.

Thank you Ronald Cohen, John Schulman, Noah Gest and friends who helped me save Papa's book collection.

Thank you Library of Congress, The Bob Dylan Archive and Mannaminne for conserving his legacy.

The warmest thanks to Jonas Ask and Hanna-Linnea Rengfors for helping me take the step from lyric to prose. And to Louise Halvardsson, you have been my steadfast companion in both words and emotion. Karin Bojs for freeing me from the quicksand when I was stuck in the insurmountable puzzle of putting the scenes in order. Thank you Karin Thunberg for reading parts of the book when it was still an embryo; you believed in my project and gave me hope. Amanda Johnsson, thank you for your hundreds of notes on photocopies of the manuscript. Thanks Jarinja for taking my desire to write seriously. Thanks Sacho and Emma, who lent me their house when I needed somewhere I could just write. Thank you everyone who supported me by reading or with kind words and encouragement through this journey.

A thousand thanks to Tor Jonasson and the staff at Salomonsson Agency for a fantastic collaboration on all fronts. Thank you, my dear editor, Sara Arvidsson. You fought beside me to the end, making everything that seemed muddy, crystal clear. A huge thanks to my publisher, Sara Nyström, for allowing *Don't Forget Me* to meet the world.

And for the English edition, a big thank you to Edward Bromberg for your great work in translating my Swedish text into English. Thank you Danny Chapman for having such a sharp editor's eye. Thank you Clare Hubbard for giving the text the final English touch. And thank you to my UK publisher Suzanne Baboneau and Simon & Schuster for bringing my work to England, taking such good care of my text.

Thank you, my two beloved children. There is nothing in this world that is more beautiful than you are.

And thank you, Papa.

2018

'So, what's going on in your life?'

He asks when I stop by the store for a cup of coffee. This is something new, him asking that. I tell him that we built a loft bed for Natasha, that Nikolai started his new school and that I'm still writing the book about him and me.

'You never told me about that,' he says.

'No, maybe not so much … I did read you a bit once, but you didn't listen.'

He says he's sorry, wonders if I'll give him a second chance. I pull my laptop from my backpack:

'Would you like me to read some for you?'

'Of course!'

Dogs hurry past on the pavement outside and I choose one of the 'nicer' passages. He sits silently and listens, wants me to read unnaturally slowly, so that he can follow every word. He listens like a child, hands resting in his lap. I pause to find another appropriate section.

'Wow, that means you understood everything, even

when you were a little girl,' he says and waits for me to find another suitable passage.

When I read about our eviction from Kocksgatan he mumbles:

'That's not the way I remember it.'

Another time he bursts out:

'Did I really do that?'

Every time I finish reading a section he looks at me sternly and demands:

'MORE!'

Half an hour later my voice is tired from reading so slowly and from holding back the tears. When I fold the laptop back into my bag he asks me what the book is going to be called.

'I think I might call it "Bye, Bye, Papa" or maybe "You Have to Live Your Own Life Too".'

'"Bye, Bye, Papa" ... Wow, that's good! That's strong. I have to sell the first copy in my window.'